Automatic Passive Income

How the Best Dividend Stocks Can Generate
Passive Income for Wealth Building.
Beginner's Guide to Investing
Andrus Istomin

I0486621

Table of
Contents

Introduction

Dividend stocks have long been a mainstay of individual investors. However, over the past few years, the investment market has become more difficult to navigate. This book is written to provide the basic dividend stock investment knowledge to the average person. To succeed as a dividend growth investor, you need to pick your dividend stocks wisely, be patient, and invest time. Only then, you can see high-quality dividend growth stocks growing at stable and sustainable rates. Dividend investing may seem like a difficult thing to understand, with the help of this book, you will get a good understanding of how it works and how you can do better with it. The book includes a lot of useful information and whether you are new to investing or dividend investment, the book will help you make sound investment decisions. This book will show you the way to get the best for your money and help achieve financial security at retirement.

Chapter One
Introduction to Dividend Investing

T imes have changed and securing financially secure retirement is not as easy as it was 30 years ago. Those days, investment returns were much more consistent than now. You could choose from a variety of investment opportunity. You could buy one of the mutual funds or invest in major public companies like General Electric or AT&T. You could have worked in a big company and know that if you work hard, you could have a secure job until you retire.

In the 1980s and 90s, you could invest in S&P 500 index fund and get regular good rates on your investment. Bad years were a rare thing these days for S&P. You could build up a nest egg inside of a 401K or IRA plan and know that is would grow about 10% each year, consistently. You could withdraw about 5% and even give yourself a raise every year in retirement to cope with inflation.

Today, it is a different scenario. After the .com bubble burst in 2000, the 9/11 attack in 2001, and the continued war in Asia, the S&P started to show weakness. During the start of the economic crisis in 2008, the S&P lost about 37% of its value. Some major US companies such as Merrill Lynch and General Motors went bankrupt. Interest rates fell to almost zero, tax revenue falls sharply, the national debt doubled, and the government had to step in to get the economy back on its feet.

The economy is turning around since then, but a secure retirement or setting aside money in a 401k plan is no longer feasible. Social security is effectively insolvent and corporations are no longer loyal to their employees. Experts saying that we have to work longer and live on just 3% of our investment portfolio during retirement.

We can no longer rely on big corporations or government to take care of us during retirement years. People who are in their 20s, 30s, 40s, and 50s need a new investment plan that offers better returns, grow consistently and provide a secure retirement.

Dividend Investing

Dividend investment stocks could allow you to live off of 4% to 6% of your portfolio each year without having to ever sell shares of stock. It is more stable than S&P 500 and has the potential to grow by 5 to 10% each year. At a first glance, it may seem there is nothing special about it, but the performance numbers will change your mind.

Standard and Poor's records S&P 500 companies that have grown their dividend every year for the last 2 decades, known as the S&P Dividend Aristocrats Index. This group includes about 52 companies and include names like Coca-Cola, Chevron, Exxon Mobil, AT&T, 3M, Wal-Mart, Procter & Gamble and McDonald's. The Indexology blog recently published a chart comparing the performance of the S&P Dividend Aristocrats Index to the performance of the S&P 500 between 1990 and 2017. These companies had cumulative returns of more than 1,900% while the return in investment in the S&P 500 resulted in cumulative returns of about 1,000%.

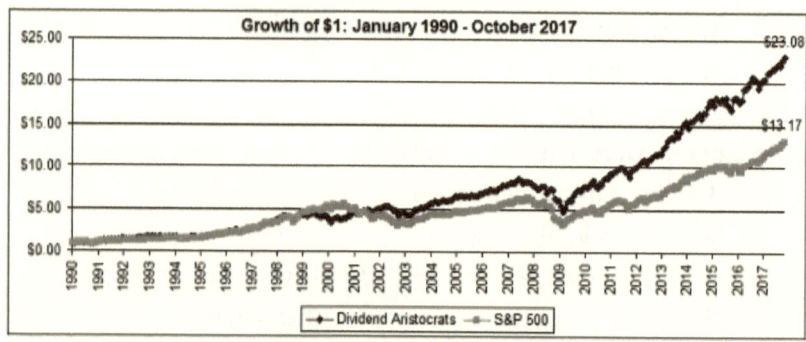

Data shows that Dividend Aristocrats has indexed about exponentially when compared to S&P 500.

Data shows that dividend investing works and you can make it work for you. You can use the power of dividend investing in your IRA, your personal 401K plan, and your individual brokerage account to create an investment portfolio of dividend growth stocks that will generate a steady income stream. It will be less volatile than the broader market and offer returns greater than the S&P 500. You can build your portfolio (with an annual yield of 4% to 6%) and will grow by 5% to 10% each year as companies raise their dividend over time. Dividend investing offers a perfect combination: growth investing and income investing. If the dividend stocks continue to perform well, you may receive 10% annual return in the upcoming years.

Our goals are same for retirement; have enough money in savings and investments so we do not have to work. For example, you may want to retire at the age of 65 or do not want to retire at all. But you want the freedom and flexibility to work part-time or take a job that pays low. If you start investing early in dividend growth stocks, at retirement you can simply stop reinvesting your dividend payments and start living off the dividend payments you receive. In some cases, you may not even have to sell any of your stock, which will allow you to leave sufficient for your children.

Earning $100,000 or more in Retirement

Let's imagine you are 35 years old, living with your spouse, have two kids. You bought a house and haven't started a retirement plan. Now, you and your spouse decide it is time to take action and start planning for your future and saving for retirement. If you and your spouse invest $12,000 per year in dividend-growth stocks (starting from the age 35 to 65). You will earn an average rate of return of 10% per year and you will receive $101,700 in dividend payments each year. You will have a total $2, 26 million in your retirement account at the age of 65. You don't have to do any other investment and you don't have to increase your saving each year.

You don't have to take a part-time job after retirement. You don't have to sell a single share of stock during retirement and you don't have to rely on your social security payments. You won't retire broke, unlike most other Americans. You will have a steady stream of cash deposits coming into your brokerage account each month from companies like Verizon, Coca-Cola, Johnson & Johnson, General Electric, Wells Fargo and Wal-Mart.

Today, the only investment strategy that stood the taste of time and offers superior returns is divided-growth investing. We already mentioned some great and trusted companies. The purpose of this book is not to recommend any specific divided stocks or company. The best way to make a profit with dividend investing is doing your own research and building a portfolio of dividend-growth companies that are promising.

Chapter two
Know Your Dividend Investing Goals

B efore starting dividend investing, you need to understand what goals you are trying to accomplish via investing, and how you want to achieve those goals. Most people depend on monthly income from their businesses or jobs. You will be in trouble for a few months if your business were to fail or you were to lose your job. The goal is to set aside money for the future as 401K and IRAs plan so that you don't have to work after retirement.

The idea of saving money for the retirement is very basic, but most people often fail to better manage their retirement fund. According to a study by GoBankingRates, 30% of Americans have no retirement saving. About 60% Americans saved only $50,000 for retirement, which is sufficient for only 1 or 2 years of retirement. Only 13% Americans have saved about $300,000 or more for retirement. If you do not want to work after retirement, then start a retirement plant and start dividend investing.

Dividend Stocks is a great investment for Retirement Investing

After you set up a 401K plan or open up an IRA, you have to decide what kind of investments you want to put your money into. For younger people, the common advice is to put money away into growth stocks that have good projections of growth as you near retirement. But growth stocks are non-ideal investments if you are in retirement. The reason is selling shares in a declining market will magnify the impacts of market losses.

For people who are close to retirement, the standard advice is to purchase a low risk, income-generating investments such as corporate bonds, municipal bonds, and treasury bills. These investments provide stability and a steady income. However, most retirees are looking to be able to safely live on at least 4% of their retirement portfolio each year, and often, the bonds and treasury bills pay a dividend of about 2%. This low income won't be enough for retirement.

Dividend stocks offer the perfect mix of income investing and growth investing. You will get a long-term capital appreciation as the stocks prices rise over time and you get immediate income in the form of dividend payments. With dividend stocks, you will be able to meet the target 4% withdrawal rate in retirement. Also, you don't have to sell any shares you own. You will never have to sell any of your shares, so you won't be affected in the event of a market dip.

Divided stocks are true passive income. You receive checks in your brokerage account or receive checks every month or quarterly basis. The only thing you have to do is keep your stocks. Your dividend payments will grow over time as companies raise their dividends on regular basis. The dividend investing isn't without risk, but the combination income they offer and the capital appreciation make them very attractive investments for your retirement.

Dividend stocks have lower volatility

Potential investors use a metric known as beta to determine the systematic risk or volatility of any given company relative to the market as a whole. The S&P 500 has a beta of 1.0. Companies that move with the market will also have a beta of less than 1 and are less volatile than the broader market (theoretically). Companies that have a beta of greater than one are more volatile than the market as a whole. Most technology stocks have a beta higher than one because they are higher-growth and higher-risk investments. Alternatively, companies that are more stable such as consumer staples, and utilities will generally have betas of less than one.

Dividend stocks have a less systematic risk and are collectively less volatile than the broader market. Most companies that pay dividends and continue to grow over them are established and profitable big companies that have a history of earnings growth. They are a more secure investment opportunity. During an economic dip, dividend stocks usually don't fall nearly as much as much younger, high-growth companies. Building a portfolio with lower volatility won't provide you better returns, but it will help you worry less. Many investors make a common mistake like selling their shares when the market is dipping to cut their losses and come back into the market when the prices gained value and prices are up. With dividend investing, you will own stocks that won't fluctuate that much and you don't have to worry about selling abruptly. Owning dividend investing gives you psychological advantages. As we mentioned before, you don't have to worry about the day-to-day value of your portfolio. Instead, you are going to focus on the perpetually growing income stream you receive in the form of dividend payments.

Dividend Stocks Outperform the Market

In 2013, J.P Morgan Asset Management issued a report (included data over a 40-year period) that showed how companies that pay dividends performed compared to companies that don't pay dividends. The report showed that companies that paid no dividends had average annual returns of just 1.6%. While companies that eliminated their dividends or lower it had average annual returns of .3%. On the other hand, companies that grew their dividends during the 40-year period saw average annual returns of 9.5%.

https://www.thestreet.com/story/13657357/1/
here-are-10-high-dividend-stocks-that-provide-20-annual-returns.htm
https://investorplace.com/2018/01/
10-dividend-stocks-that-will-deliver-double-digit-returns-every-year/

It is not surprising that companies that pay and grow their dividends outperformed the companies that don't. Data shows that 40% of returns of the S&P 500 over the last 80 years have come from dividend payments. Data shows that between 1926 and 2007, reinvested dividend income accounted for approximately 95% of the compound long-term return earned by compound by companies in the S&P 500 (**http://www.etf.com/publications/journalofindexes/ joi-articles/3869-the-imporance-of-investment-income.html**).

S&P 500 DIVIDEND ARISTOCRATS INDEX
GROWTH OF $100,000 SINCE INCEPTION (MAY 2005 - SEPT 2017)

The S&P 500 Dividend Aristocrats Index is more proof the companies that pay strong dividends regularly outperform the market. During the last 10-year period ending in September 2017, the S&P 500 index had an average annualized return of 11% with dividends reinvested. During the same period, Dividend Aristocrats Index returned an average annulled return of 16%. The Dividend-paying stocks have outperformed the broader market by 4 to 5% every year.

There is no scam in Dividend Payments

The earnings numbers announced by publicly traded companies are mainly a product of accounting and often do not truly reflect the company's actual financial health. Unscrupulous executives and experienced accountants can make a bad company look like financially stable on paper. A good example is Enron, in the 1990s, the company financials looked great on paper. However, behind the scenes, there was another story. So, accounting numbers can be manipulated, but remember, dividend payments can't be faked. Either a dividend payment appears in a company's shareholder's brokerage account or it does n't. There are no tricks to make dividend payments look stronger than it actually is. Also, a company that can pay dividend payments indicates that it has enough money to make its dividend payments. However, paying dividend payments doesn't necessarily mean that company has strong cash flow because companies will occasionally borrow money to pay their dividend during cyclical downturns. However, even those companies are financially on sound footing and this is why they are able to borrow money.

Healthy Companies pay Dividend

Companies that pay dividend regularly tend to be very healthy financially. Having new money coming into the company is one of the best signs of a company's overall health. Only financially secure companies can pay a dividend for a long period of time. Healthy companies don't launch speculative growth projects or can't carelessly acquire companies like companies that do not pay dividends.

Dividend Stocks will protect you against inflation

Dividend-growth stocks offer you a better protection against inflation than other fixed-income investments such as bonds. Most bonds pay a fixed rate through its maturity. The problem is, during inflationary periods, each successive interest payment that you receive has less purchasing power than the last. The value of your bonds will decline because of the inflation to match the bond marketer's current rates.

No, the dividend stocks are not immune to the effects of inflation. However, publically traded companies can counteract it by raising their prices to match inflation. Data shows that S&P 500 has grown at an annual rate of 4.12% between 1912 and 2005. On the other hand, the consumer price index has risen by 3.3% annually during the same period. The consumer price index is an accepted measure of inflation.

So, as long as a company grows their dividend at the same or a faster rate, shareholders' dividend payment won't lose any purchasing power.

Risks of Investing in Dividend Stocks

Dividend stocks aren't without risk either. There are a few investment risks associated with dividend stocks. Let's discuss them:

- Task Policy Risk: under the current U.S. tax code, dividends receive preferable tax treatment. Qualified dividend payments are taxed at capital-gains rates. Once the interest rates offered by risk-free dividend investments rise, dividend stocks become less attractive compared to other investment options. As interest rates rise, outflows from the dividend stocks will lower their share price and drive up the yield of dividend stocks.

- Risk of price volatility: similar to publically traded companies, the dividend stocks have the same risks. As market conditions change, their prices will fluctuate. Usually, stocks perform well over the course of long-term; so therefore, the investors must be prepared for share price decline. Be aware, you might have to cope with 30% decline in the price of your dividend stocks.

- Risk of Dividend Payment Cuts: companies that are facing difficulties will have problems making dividend payments. Some companies may decide to cut its dividend eventually. You need to monitor your companies in your portfolio. If any company's dividend appears unsustainable, then it might be time to get out.

Wrap-Up: the most important matter in dividend investment is risk-adjusted after-tax performance. In other words, how much money I am getting after taxes at the end of the day. We know that dividend stocks are less volatile and have lower systematic risk than other publicly traded companies. We also know that dividend stocks outperformed the S&P 500 and other asset classes over the last few decades. Dividend payments also receive preferential tax treatment under current U.S. tax law.

Chapter three
Fundamentals of Dividend Investing

I t is easy to think of dividends, stocks, and other financial concepts as abstract terms that are not related to the real world. If you were to buy shares of Johnson & Johnson, you would become a minority owner of that company. You and other shareholders of Johnson & Johnson vote to elect a board of directors. When the company makes a profit, the board decides what to do with the money at the end of each quarter. They can reinvest it into the business, they can hold on to it as retained earnings or they can decide to return it to their shareholders in the form a dividend payment. When the company decides to distribute the part of the company's profit in the form of a dividend, you are entitled to your share of the profit distribution as a part-owner in the company. Once you receive it, you can reinvest the dividend payment and earn more shares or spend the money.

How Dividend Payouts Work

Hundreds of millions of dollars in shares of large companies are bought and sold every day and it is not easy to determine which shareholders are entitled to receive a dividend payment. For example, if you bought shares of Johnson & Johnson after a dividend was declared (but before it was paid out), the question is who will get the dividend, you or the previous owner? Here are a few important dates to remember:

- Declaration Date: the dividend declaration date is the date that a company's board of directors publicly announces the next dividend. This date has no impact on who will receive the dividend payment.
- Ex-Dividend Date: this date is the day on which any new shares that are bought or sold are no longer eligible to receive the next scheduled dividend. If you want to receive the next dividend payment, you must buy your shares that day before the market closes. The ex-dividend date makes it easier for a company to reconcile which shareholders are eligible to receive a dividend payment.
- Record date: shareholders must properly record their ownership on or before the record date to receive a dividend payment. Those who do not register their ownership will not receive a dividend payment. In the US and other countries, registration is automatic so you don't have to worry about it.
- Payable date: on the payable date, the dividend payments will actually be credited to shareholders brokerage account or mailed to them.

DIVIDEND CAPTURE STRATEGIES

The ex-dividend date is the day that determines who receives a dividend payment. Some clever people might try to game the system by owning the shares during the ex-dividend date (buying them the previous date) and make a profit. This strategy seems a great idea to make a profit, but it almost never works in practice. When a company goes ex-dividend, its stock price will usually lower by a dollar amount roughly equivalent to the amount of the dividend paid. This natural adjustment prevents people from trying to game the dividend system and capture dividend payments without owning a stock for more than one day at a time. Dividend capture strategies are very difficult to time and rarely work.

Why Companies Pay Dividends

Companies that are growing rapidly want to put most of their cash flow from earnings back into growing the company and this is why they don't pay dividends. Fast-growing companies may use earnings to buy out another company, fund other growth projects, start a new division or purchase new assets. This is the reason many companies such as Google and Amazon. Moreover, established companies may not pay dividends because of their belief that they can create more shareholder value by reinvesting their earnings. This is the reason why Berkshire Hathway does not pay a dividend. However, they invest in dividend-paying stocks, such as General Motors, IBM, Coco-Coal and Wells Fargo.

Mature and established companies do not need to reinvest like high growth companies. If mature companies have excess earnings, they may decide to pay dividends. Mature companies will often pay dividends to attract and drive up the price of their stock, attract new shareholders or to create greater demand for their stock.

Regular Vs Special Dividends

Regular payments are made on a set schedule, such as every month or every quarter. Most publicly traded companies will pay dividends quarterly basis. Some ETFs, stocks and mutual funds will pay monthly. Some international companies pay dividends only once or twice every year. Almost all of the dividends that you receive will be regular dividend payments. Special dividends are one-time payments made to shareholders when a company finds itself with excess cash or asset.

Types of Dividend Payments

Usually, dividend payments are provided to shareholders in the form of cash, but there are several types of dividend payments, including:

- Cash Dividends: cash dividends are by far the most common type of dividend and will account for the vast majority of the dividend payments you receive. Cash dividends are simply a transfer of your share of a company's earnings to your brokerage account in the form of cash.
- Stock dividends: issuing of new shares of stock to existing shareholders is known as stock dividends. For example, you own 10,000 shares and the company decided to pay a 5% stock dividend, you would receive 500 new shares of the company. The stock dividends do not increase the value of the company.
- Property Dividends: companies may issue non-monetary dividends to their shareholders. A property dividend could come in the form of physical assets such as inventories the company holds, or shares of a subsidiary company. The property dividends are recorded at the value of the assets provided to shareholders for tax purposes.
- Scrip Dividends: a company may issue a scrip dividend when it does not have enough money to make dividend payments. A scrip dividend is a promissory note to pay shareholders a cash dividend in the future.
- Liquidating Dividends: a liquidating dividend is a return of the capital that was originally contributed by shareholders. This type of dividend happened when a company is shutting down.

In most cases, you will receive cash dividends and occasionally, you will get a stock dividend.

Types of Dividend Stocks

Companies such as General Electric and Johnson & Johnson give stocks as a dividend. There are actually many different types of dividend-paying publicly traded companies that operate in different industries, have different tax liabilities, have different corporate structures, and have other characteristics that you should be aware of.

Consumer Staples

Companies that sell products that consumers use from day-to-day, such as personal products, household products, beverages, and tobacco are known as consumer staples. Unilever, Philip Morris, Coca-Cola, Proctor, and Gamble are examples of consumer-staples companies. Consumer staples companies sell products that consumers still need to buy during an economic recession. Because of this reason, these companies have consistent earnings and cash flow. Usually, these companies are very well established generally pay dividends.

Bank	Forward Dividend Yield
New York Community Bancorp	4.33%
People's United Financial	3.72%
Wells Fargo	2.90%
BB&T	2.73%
Huntington Bancshares	2.62%
S&P 500	2.17%

DATA SOURCE YCHARTS.COM THE WALL STREET JOURNAL

BANKS

Before the economic recession during 2008 and 2009, many large banks were established dividend payers and offered yields between 3% and 5%. During the last few years, some of the large banks have slowly started raising their dividend payments again and some are currently paying dividend yields between 1.5% to 3%.

Energy Companies

Large-cap energy companies such as ExxonMobil, Chevron, and British Petroleum have a history of paying strong dividends. The dividend from raise and fail with the price of crude oil. Master limited partnerships are a subset of energy companies that are structured as publicly traded limited partnerships. Investors who buy shares of MLPs become limited partners in the business and the company is run by its general partners. The MLP structure is used almost exclusively for energy and utility companies. MLPs tend to own terminals and energy pipelines. This makes them less sensitive to energy prices than large-cap energy production companies are. MLPs have constant cash flow and this allows them to pay handsome dividends. MLPs can give dividend between 5% and 8%.

Examples of MLPs include Enterprise Products Partners, Magellan Midstream Partners and Spectra Energy Partners.

Royalty Trusts

Royalty trusts, like master limited partnerships, invest in assets in the energy sector. Royalty trusts produce income from the production of natural resources like natural gas, oil, and coal. Royalty trusts are simply publicly financing vehicles that allow large energy production companies to lease natural resource assets. Royalty trusts are operated by banks, which take care of their paperwork, manage their financial interests and make distributions to shareholders. Royalty trusts cash flow and distributions can swing wildly as commodity prices and production levels change.

The San Juan Basin Royalty Trust is the largest royalty trust in the U.S. The trust owns oil and natural gas resources in the San Juan Basin of northwestern New Mexico. Many Royalty trusts pay very high dividend yields, often in excess of 10%. Royalty trusts also have some unique tax benefits. A wild swing in energy prices could dramatically change the value of your investment in a royalty trust. If you choose to invest in a royalty trust, prepare for a wild ride.

Utilities

Utility companies tend to be very stable and predictable business that generates strong cash flow. Consumers will always need home heating oil, propane, natural gas, electricity, and water to provide for their basic needs. This is why utility companies tend to cope well with an economic downturn. Utility companies have huge infrastructure requirements and can use the same infrastructure for decades. Utilities get area monopoly and this is why they are heavily regulated. State agencies establish standardized rates that utilities can charge for water, electricity and natural gas to prevent the abuse of monopoly power. Utility companies currently pay dividend yields between 3% and 6%. Examples of large utility companies include Pacific Gas and Electric, American Electric Power, National Grid Plc, and Duke Energy Corp.

Real-Estate Investment Trusts

Real-estate investment trusts are a special type of corporate entity used to own and operate income-producing commercial real estates, such as hospitals, warehouses, hotels, malls, restaurants and various types of medical facilities. REITs can be privately held or can be publicly traded. REITs are required by law to pay out 90% of their earnings as dividends to their shareholders. This means they tend to offer above-average dividend yields. Examples of REITs include Avalon Bay Companies, Public Storage, Welltower, Ventas, and Simon Property Group.

Preferred Stocks

Preferred stocks are a special classification of stock ownership that has a higher priority claim on company earnings, assets, and dividend payments that common stock does. Preferred stockholders generally receive higher dividend yields than common stockholders. However, the dividend payments on preferred stock are fixed and will not grow over time. Preferred Stocks said to have features of both bonds and stocks because they offer fixed-income payments and also offer some opportunity for capital appreciation. Preferred-stock mutual funds and ETFs usually pay dividend yields between 5% and 8% in today's market.

Business development companies have very specific legal requirements under the investment company Act that they must follow. Many dividend investors avoid investing in BDCs because of their wild volatility and inconsistent payout amounts.

Chapter Four
Choosing Dividend Stocks

C hoosing right dividend stocks aren't as easy as picking the companies that pay the highest dividend yields. Companies that pay a dividend four or five times greater than the dividend yield of the S&P 500 are not going to last long. You may be tempted to purchase stocks of the companies that offer 7% or more dividend yields, but these high yields are often the result of weak earnings and a significant drop in a company's share that cannot support the company's dividend over the long term.

As an income investor, your goal is to get the best yield available on your money and this can make you focus on dividend yield alone. However, you need to consider several other criteria before buying dividend stocks. You need to look at important financial metrics such as a company's dividend payout ratio, return on equity, net margins, and debt. You need to determine if the dividend is likely to grow in the future by the company's expected future earnings growth and its history of raising its dividend. You also need to know the price you are paying is fair. Let's discuss the criteria for buying dividend stock.

Dividend Yield

The dividend yield is the measure of what percentage of a company's current share price is paid out in dividends each year. A company's dividend yield will fluctuate throughout the day as the price of the company stock rises and falls with the market. Let's imagine that there is a company named X that has a share price of $100 and it pays an annual dividend of $2.50. If the X company's share price were to rise to $150.00 and its dividend does not change at $2.50 per share, then the company's dividend yield would fall to 1.67%. If the price of stocks drops, the company's dividend yield will rise. If the company were to post dismal earnings and its share price dropped to $50.00, its dividend yield would rise to 5.0%.

Focus on publicly traded companies that pay a dividend at least 50% higher than that of the S&P 500. Focusing on companies that pay a significantly higher yield than the broad-market indexes. You should treat companies that pay an unusually high dividend yield with skepticism. If a company's dividend yield is more than three times greater than the dividend yield of the S&P 500, do research before investing. You should evaluate a company that pays of 6.15% or higher with an extra amount of caution. Companies that pay extremely high dividend yields often come with massive investment risks. However, it doesn't mean that you should avoid dividend stocks with high yields totally. Ideally, you should focus on companies that pay dividend yields between 3.5% and 6.5%.

HISTORY OF DIVIDEND Growth

After the dividend yield, you should look at the history of dividend payments. How many years in a row has the company raised its dividend? How much does the company raise its dividend every year, on average? Has the company ever cut its dividend during a recession? Essentially, we are looking for reliable dividend payments that have the potential to grow over time regardless of current market conditions. If a company has a track record of raising its dividend every year for the last 20 years, then there is a strong likelihood that it will continue to yield strong dividend.

When analyzing, look at what happened to the company during the great recession of 2008 and 2009. During that period, 82 S&P 500 companies were able to raise their dividend while 46 companies reduced or eliminated their quarterly dividend payments. If a company was able to maintain and grow its dividend during 2008 and 2009, then, it is a good sign the company is committed to its dividend and will pay a dividend in challenging times.

Focus on companies that have raised their dividend every year for the last 10 years. If a company has raised its dividend 10 years in a row, it is a good indication that the company is committed to growing its annual dividend. Read what company management has to say about company's future growth. Also, focus on companies that have grown their dividend by an average of 5% to 10% over the last three years. For that company that has a dividend yield of less than 4%, look for an annual dividend-growth rate very close to 10%. You can use MarketBeat.com to look up a company's dividend yield, its annual dividend, its dividend payout ratio, its forward-looking dividend payout ratio, its track record of consecutive years of dividend growth, its 3-year average of annual dividend growth and other important financial metrics.

Earnings Growth and Dividend Payout Ratio

Dividends are paid to shareholders out of earnings. If a company's earnings are stagnant on a year-over-year basis, the company may not raise its dividend at all or may issue a token dividend increase to maintain its track record of consecutively raising dividends every year. If a company's earnings decline for several quarters in a row and it must pay out an unsustainably high percentage of its earnings as dividends, its board of directors may be forced to lower or eliminate its dividend.

Dividend payout ratio is calculated by taking the company's annual dividend and dividing it by its earnings per share. You should also calculate a company's forward-looking dividend payout ratio by dividing an average of analysts' EPS estimates for the next fiscal year by its dividend. The companies that you invest in as a dividend investor will generally have a relatively high dividend payout ratio. Focus on investing in companies that have dividend payout ratios between 405 and 70%. Avoid companies that have a payout ratio higher than 75%, because there isn't a lot of money left over to reinvest in the growth of the business. However, a very high payout ratio does not mean a company will automatically cut its dividend. Master limited partnerships, business development companies and real estate investment trusts are the two exceptions to the suggested 75% dividend payout ratio limit. BDCs and REITs are required by law to pay out 90% of their income to shareholders in the form of a dividend. When evaluating the sustainability of dividend payments for MLPs and REITs, calculate a company's payout ratio based on its distributable cash flow rather than its reported earnings. Distributable cash flow is a measure of profitability that identifies how much money the company actually has to use for paying out dividends, reducing debt, investing in growth or buying back its own shares.

Debt

Banks will rarely lend more money to people that are already deeply in debt. Likewise, publically traded companies that have a large amount of debt are often limited in their ability to return capital to shareholders in the form of dividends because much of their cash flow goes toward making a debt payment. By looking at its debt-to-equity ratio, you can determine a publicly traded company's debt burden. The debt-to-equity ratio is simply the amount of debt that the company has divided by the amount of shareholder equity. A debt-to-equity ratio of 1:1 is good and anything lower is even better. When evaluating a company's debt-to-equity ratio, make sure to compare it to the debt-to-equity ratios to other companies in the same industry so that you are making a true comparison of how much debt a company has compared to its competitors.

Profitability

Looking at the company's net profit margins is a good way to determine whether or not a company will continue to have the free cash flow to pay its dividend. Net profit margins are shorted as net margins. Net margin is a metric that calculates the percentage of a company's net revenue that is kept as profit. Companies that have higher net margins are able to weather economic ups and downs easier than companies with lower net margins because they are better temporarily weather periods of lower sales or higher expenses.

Profit margins will vary significantly from industry to industry, so there is no hard-and-fast rule indicating what would be considered a healthy net margin for any given dividend stock. However, you should demand minimum net margins of at least 5% in the companies that you invest in, because net margins can vary depending on current economic conditions. By requiring a minimum level of profitability, you can avoid relying on getting dividend payments from companies whose ability to generate profit during challenging economic conditions is in question. ROE or return on equity is another way to measure a company's profitability. ROE can be calculated by dividing a company's net income by the company's shareholder equity. ROE shows the percentage of net income that a company is generating relative to the amount of money that shareholders have invested in the company. Companies that have a higher ROE percentage are more efficient in utilizing their shareholder equity to generate returns for their shareholders. Generally speaking, analysts consider a 15-20% ROE percentage as good. You can use YCharts.com to look up a company's net margins, historical debt-to-equality ratios, and return-on-equity numbers.

Fair Value Estimate

There is an inverse correlation between a company's share price and its dividend yield. This makes it especially important to pay attention to the ups and downs of the market and by companies when their share price is down, they have been beaten up a little and their dividend yield is higher than usual. **www.morning-star.com**[1] is a good tool to determine where a company is trading relative to its intrinsic. Morning star's fair value estimates are far from a perfect metric because all equities research analysts are fallible, but they can provide a helpful idea whether or not a stock has been overbought or oversold. Another way is by looking at a chart of the company's dividend yield over time. By looking at a graphic representation of the company's annual dividend relative to its share price over a period of several years, you can see whether the company's dividend is currently higher or lower than its historical average. Dividend.com is a useful website to chart a company's dividend yield.

Example: The Dividend Discount Model

- Suppose that a stock will pay three annual dividends of $200 per year, and the appropriate risk-adjusted discount rate, k, is 8%. Terminal price $ 1200.
- In this case, what is the value of the stock today?

$$V(0) = \frac{D(1)}{(1+k)} + \frac{D(2)}{(1+k)^2} + \frac{D(3)}{(1+k)^3} + \frac{P(3)}{(1+k)^3}$$

$$V(0) = \frac{\$200}{(1+0.08)} + \frac{\$200}{(1+0.08)^2} + \frac{\$200}{(1+0.08)^3} + \frac{\$1,200}{(1+0.08)^3} = \$1,468.01$$

---

1.   http://www.morning-star.com

$$P_0 = \frac{D_1}{K_e - g}$$

$D_1 = $ *Expected Dividend for Year 1*

$g = $ *Growth Rate*

$K_e = $ *Discount rate*

USING DIVIDEND DISCOUNT Model to Develop a Fair Value Estimate

DDMS or Dividend Discount Models attempt to identify a fair price for a stock based on the expected future dividends that shareholders will receive. The theory is that capital gains and volatility in share price are the results of investors adjusting their expectations from a company's future stream of dividend income. DDMs attempt to project the value of all future dividends and then discount them to a net present value that identifies a fair value for the company's current share price.

The simplified form of a dividend discount model can be helpful in identifying a fair price to pay for a stock. However, you should be cautious about how much attention you pay to DDM calculations. We may not have a good idea of what the company's cost of capital actually is and what the company's long-term average annual dividend-growth rate will be.

Economic Moats

An economic moat describes certain advantages that some companies have that allow them to stay ahead of the competition. The larger the moat a company has, the more likely that is will continue to be a profitable and viable business in the years to come. There are several types of competitive advantages that can create an economic moat for a company:

- Barriers to Entry: some industries have high regulatory or financial barriers to entry that would make it extremely difficult for new competitors to enter the market. For example, it would be almost impossible to create a new railroad network in the U.S. because it would take a massive land acquiring from private property owners. The current railroad owners have huge economic moats because it is highly unlikely that there will be any new rail lines in the U.S.
- Brand Name: studies show that consumers are more likely to buy from brand names than from an unknown company. For example, the brand Coca-Cola is so ingrained in the minds of consumers, no other brands can unseat it.
- Economies of Scale: companies that produce, transport and sell goods at a larger scale can often benefit from reduced costs compared to their competitors. Wal-Mart is a perfect example of massive scale. Wal-Mart sells nearly $500 billion per year with its 4,000 stores. They can sell products at a cheaper price and make higher profits.
- High Switching Costs: if it takes a significant amount of time, money or effort for a customer to switch from one company to another, consumers are much less likely to change brand. For example, people rarely switch banks because it takes a lot of work to set up new accounts.

Economic moats can sometimes be difficult to quantify or assign an economic value to, but having any of these competitive advantages is preferable to not having them at all.

Dividend Analysis Example

Let's start with Verizon. The company currently pays a dividend yield of 4.27%, which is a satisfactory rate.

Dividend Evaluation Checklist

- Dividend Yield: ideally between 3.5 and 6.5%.
- A number of consecutive years of Dividend Growth: ideally at least 10.
- Average Annual Dividend Growth: ideally between 5% and 10%.
- Average Annual Earnings Growth: ideally in line with or above dividend-growth rates.
- Dividend Payout Ratio: ideally less than 75%, except for REITs and MLPs.
- Debt to Equity Ratio: ideally 1:1 or less
- Net Margins: ideally at least 5%
- Return on equity: ideally at least 10%
- Fair Value Estimate: ideally trading below Morning star's fair value estimate

Chapter Five
Buying that Perfect Dividend

Fortunately, there are now several tools, websites, and lists that can help dividend investors to make their dividend stock sale.

Dividend Lists

Over the last several decades, NASDAQ, Standard and Poor's and a number of other companies have attempted to create models that identify best-of-breed dividend stocks. Each of these stock lists has specific requirements for companies to be listed, having a certain minimum market cap, having raised their dividend every year for a minimum number of years, and meeting specific capital requirements. These lists, such as the S&P Dividend Aristocrats provide a good starting point for anyone looking to create a portfolio of dividend stocks.

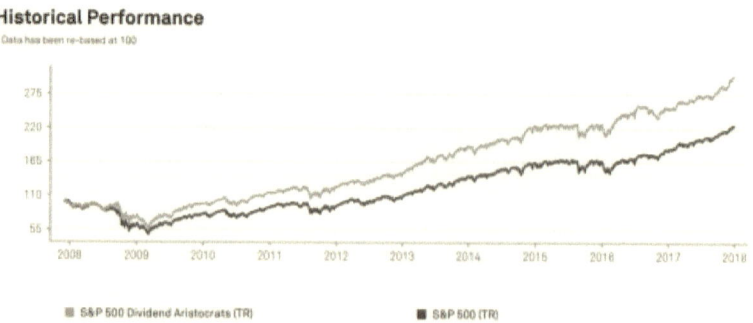

Historical Performance
* Data has been re-based at 100

■ S&P 500 Dividend Aristocrats (TR)   ■ S&P 500 (TR)

S&P Dividend Aristocrats

The S&P Dividend Aristocrats list is a list of S&P 500 companies that have raised their dividend every year for at least the last 25 years.

Companies must have an average daily trading volume of $5 million and have a minimum market cap of $3 billion.

The reasons that the S&P 500 Dividend Aristocrats Index dramatically outperformed the S&P 500 Index over the last decade are, firstly, companies that pay strong dividends are likely to be generating strong earnings and cash flow that support their above-average dividend payments. Second, a company that pays dividends has to be more selective about how they reinvest earnings into their businesses.

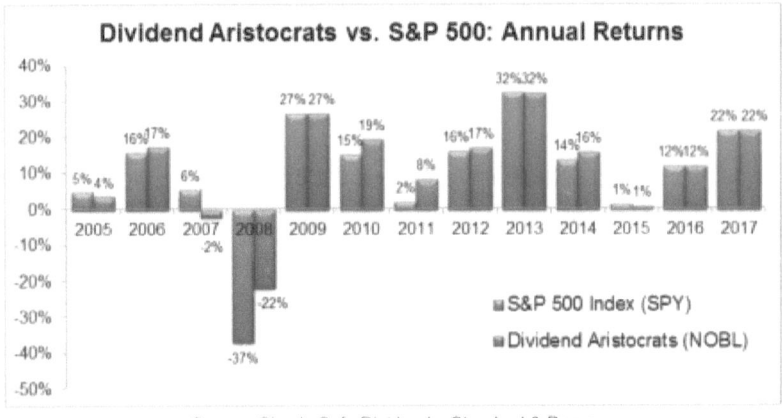

Source: Simply Safe Dividends, Standard & Poors

Because a portion of the company's cash flow is paid out in dividends. Finally, many would agree that the companies listed in the S&P Dividend Aristocrats Index are simply higher-quality companies on average. For a company to have the earnings and cash flow to support increasing its dividend for 25 consecutive years, it must have an economic moat or another competitive advantage that allows it to outperform its competitors. This link (**https://www.suredividend.com/dividend-aristocrats-list/**) will give you more information on S&P Dividend Aristocrats.

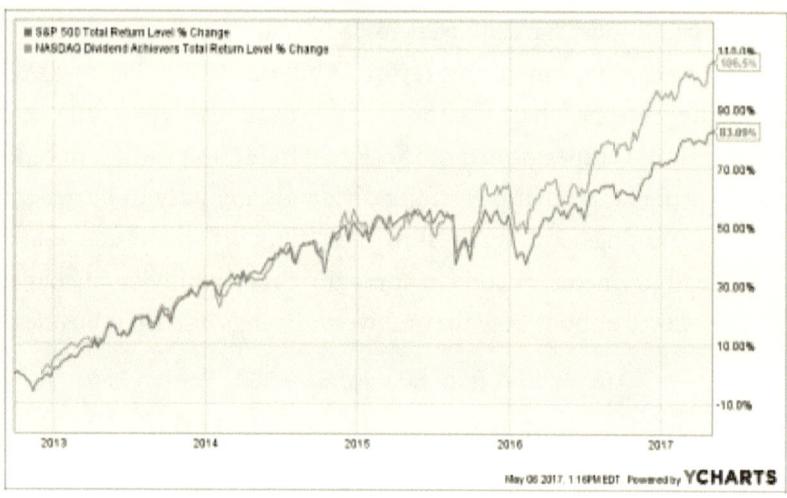

NASDAQ Dividend Achievers Index

The NASDAQ Dividend Achievers Index is a list of 274 companies that have raised their dividend each year for at least the last 10 years. To be included in the Dividend Achievers Index, a company must be a member of the NASDAQ US Benchmark Index and meet certain minimum capitalization and liquidity requirements. You can view a list of companies that are currently included in the Dividend Achievers Index at **www.marketbeat.com/dividends/achievers/**[1]. The companies listed in the Dividend Achievers Index have similar qualities to the companies listed in the S&P 500 Dividend Aristocrats Index. The major difference is that the companies in the Dividend Achievers Index do not have a long of a record of accomplishment of raising their dividends as those in the Dividend Aristocrats Index do. It may be tempting to focus exclusively on the companies that are in the Dividend Aristocrats Index because of their long track records, but it can be a mistake.

David Fish's Dividend Champions List

Like the S&P Dividend Aristocrats Index, the Dividend Champions list is a list of companies that have raised their dividends

---

1.   http://www.marketbeat.com/dividends/achievers/

for 25 consecutive years. (**www.DirectInvesting.com**[2].) The major difference between the two indexes is that the Dividend Champions list does not include the capital and liquidity requirements of Dividend Aristocrats Index.

Dividend Kings

The Dividend Kings list includes companies that have raised their dividend every year for more than 50 consecutive years. From this link (**https://www.suredividend.com/dividend-kings/**) you can view the list.

Cautions

These lists mentioned in this chapter are a good starting point for your research. However, do not buy a stock just because it is included in a list. Dividend lists are a good place to start looking for companies to invest in, and make sure that the dividend stocks you buy meet the other recommended criteria.

2.   http://www.DirectInvesting.com

Chapter Six
Income Tax on Dividend Stocks

Let's imagine that you are considering four different investments that all pay a 4.5% dividend yield. A real-estate-investment trust, a master limited partnership, a municipal-bond fund, and a blue-chip dividend stock. Dividends from a blue-chip stock are taxed at capital-gains rates and the after-tax yield will be 3.825% (if your capital gains are taxed at 15%). The MLP will also generate an after-tax yield of 3.825%. The REIT is taxed at your normal tax rate. The percentage difference may not seem that different. However, if you have a $1 million investment portfolio, the difference could be $45,000 per year in retirement and $32,400 in retirement.

Learning how specific types of investments are taxed is extremely important because of the uneven tax burden that is placed on different types of investment income.

History Dividend Taxes

Before 2003, qualified dividends were taxed at the same rates as ordinary income. After 2003, the Congress lowers the dividend tax and make the dividend tax rate the same as the capital-gains tax rate. After 2010, via a compromise in the Congress, most households were able to maintain their lower tax rates. The lone exception was individuals that made more than $400,000 per year or families that made more than $450,000 per year, whose top tax rate rose from 35% to 39.6%. Individuals and families in the top tax rate would pay a new capital gains and dividend rate of 20%, up from 15% previously.

Under today's tax code, filers in the 10% and 15% brackets pay no tax on their qualified dividend income. Most individuals pay 15% tax on dividend income and filers in the top tax bracket pay a 20% tax rate on qualified dividend income rates. In addition to the normal dividend tax, the Affordable Care Act of 2012 instituted a new 3.8% net investment income tax that applies to dividends, capital gains and other kinds of passive investment income which is charge to single filers that make more than $200,000 per year and joint filers that more than $250,000 per year. This means that you could pay a dividend tax rate as low as zero if you don't have much income or a dividend tax rate as high as 23.8% if you are in the top tax bracket.

Qualified Dividends

In order for a dividend payment to be considered a qualified dividend and be taxed at a preferential capital-gains rate, it must meet a few basic criteria. The dividend payment must have been paid by an American or a foreign qualifying company. A foreign corporation is considered qualified if it is incorporated in the US, it is eligible for the benefits of a comprehensive income tax treaty with the U.S. or if the stock is readily tradable on an established securities market in the U.S.

There are some types of dividend payments that are explicitly excluded from receiving qualified dividend rates. Dividends paid by real estate investment trusts (REITs), master limited partnerships (MLPs), employee stock options, tax-except companies, and money market accounts do not receive qualified dividend treatment and are taxed as ordinary income. Special one-time dividends also do not receive qualified dividend treatment. These rules may sound complicated, but most dividends that you receive by investing in companies like General Electric, Coca-Cola, AT&T, Apple, and

Wal-Mart will be qualified dividends as long as you are not regularly trading in and out of positions.

International Stocks

You may look to international dividend stocks to add to your portfolio. There are many companies outside of the US that offer consistent dividend payments and dividend growth. Many foreign countries see dividend payments to international investors as an easy source of tax revenue and charge foreign investors dividend tax rates between 5% and 30% on dividend payments. Some countries such as the UK and Argentina do not tax dividends paid to US investors due to various tax treaties that the U.S. has with those countries. Here (**https://seekingalpha.com/article/ 248039-withholding-tax-rates-by-country-for-foreign-stock-dividends**) is a link to international dividend tax rates by country.

Fortunately, there may be a way to recoup some or all of the taxes collected on your dividend payments by foreign credits. The U.S. tax code includes a credit for tax payments made to foreign governments, known as the foreign tax credit. The goal is not to tax you twice. Regulations regarding the foreign tax credit are complex, so check with a qualified financial professional if you plan to take the foreign tax credit.

Other than tax considerations, you should also consider political risks, currency risks, and regulatory risks before investing in foreign dividend stocks. Natural disasters, war, terrorism can significantly change the economic outlook of a country and the economic outlook of companies that operate within its borders.

Another important consideration regarding investing in international dividend stocks in that they often do not mirror the monthly or quarterly payment schedules that are common in U.S. dividend stocks. Some foreign stocks will also vary the amount of their dividend based on the company's actual profits. If you are considering buying a foreign dividend stock and what to place a trade, you may find

AUTOMATIC PASSIVE INCOME - HOW THE BEST DIVIDEND STOCKS CAN GENERATE PASSIVE INCOME FOR WEALTH BUILDING.

39

out that you aren't able to place trades on many exchanges outside the U.S. in your brokerage account.

TAXATION OF REAL-ESTATE Investment Trusts

Real estate investment trusts are a special type of corporate entity used for commercial real-estate projects that can avoid paying corporate taxes at the federal level. REITs have special requirements under the tax code because they are not set up as a typical Corporation like most publicly traded companies are. REITs have the same accounting and valuations that corporations do, but instead of distributing profits to shareholders, they distribute cash flow. The IRS requires REITs to pay out 90% of their income to shareholders ad distributions. When a REIT meets the 90% payout requirement, it is generally all exempted from paying corporate taxes at the federal level. Because of this tax provision, distributions from REITs are not considered qualified dividends and are taxed at a shareholder's ordinary income rates. A portion of a REITs distribution may also be considered a non-taxable return of capital, which reduces a shareholder's taxable income in the year it is received and defers payment of taxes on that portion of the investor's shares until they are sold.

The tax treatment of REIT distributions can make them less attractive to investors in high tax brackets. If you are in the top tax bracket, you will pay your ordinary tax rate of 39.9% plus the net investment income tax of 3.8% on any distributions you receive from a REIT. When possible, hold your REIT investments in a non-taxable or tax-advantaged investment account, such as a 401K or IRA to avoid paying ordinary income taxes on REITs.

Master Limited partnerships (MLPs)

Master Limited Partnerships (MLPs) are a special type of corporate entity that is a combination of a partnership and a publicly traded company. They are primarily used as corporate vehicles for energy and utility companies. Since MLPs are pass-through entities, their income is only taxed at the level of the partners in the MLP and is generally not subject to corporate taxes at the federal level. While MLPs offer significant tax benefits to investors, there are two caveats to be aware of. First, you should not invest in an MLP through an IRA or another tax-deferred account. Income from an MLP is not tax-deferred if shares are held in an IRA. Second, investing in MLPs may make filing your taxes each year slightly more complicated. You will receive a K-1 form at the end of the year, instead of a 1099 form.

Taxation of Preferred Stocks

Preferred stocks are a special class of shares in a company that pays a fixed dividend yield like a bond does. The tax treatment of dividends paid by preferred stocks can vary from security to security. Some preferred stocks will pay out qualified dividends just as any other publicly traded company. Divided payments issued by trust-preferred securities are not qualified dividend because they are essentially interest payments. Preferred-stock dividends issued by business development companies are also not qualified distributions. The preferred-stock issue's prospectus will explain the tax treatment of the stock along with other important investment information.

Taxation of Royalty Income Trusts

Royalty income trusts are a special type of entity that oil and natural gas producers use to provide a secure financing source for the operations of their businesses. Royalty trusts generate income from the production of natural resources, such as oil, coal and natural gas. Royalty Trusts exist strictly to won natural-resource assets and receive royalties from the companies that are harvesting the natural resources they own. Royalty trusts tend to have very high yields because they are required to pay out virtually all of their cash flow as distributions. Similar to MLPs, royalty trusts are considered pass-through vehicles and are not subject to corporate tax at the federal level. When an investor in a royalty trust sells their interest, they will be taxed at their capital gains rate based on their final cost basis and the current price of the royalty trust. Investors in royalty trusts may be able to claim unusual tax credits, such as receiving a credit for producing fuel from unconventional sources. These credits usually don't amount to much.

Taxation of Business Development companies

Business development companies are a special type of corporate entity that was created by Congress in 1980 to encourage public investment in privately held companies. Like others, business development companies are pass-through entities and are not taxed at the corporate level if they pay out 90% of their taxable income every year and derive more than 90% of their income from capital gains, dividends, and interest on securities. Just like with REITs, distributions paid by BDCs are taxed at an investor's ordinary income rates and not considered qualified dividends. For this reason, BDCs are best held in tax-advantaged accounts like self-directed 401K and IRAs.

Invest in Dividend Stocks using your IRA

Your first investment priority at the beginning of each year should be maxing out your individual retirement accounts, your 401K/403B plan and any other tax-advantaged investment accounts you may have. Taxes on dividends and capital gains can eat up a significant portion of your investment income when you use a standard brokerage account. So, always max out your tax-advantaged investment options before investing through a traditional taxable brokerage account.

There are two distinct types of IRAs. Traditional IRAs allow investors to receive an immediate tax deduction for contributions made to an IRA. However, you will have to pay your ordinary income tax rate on any money you withdraw from your IRA during retirement. Roth IRAs do not offer an up-front tax deduction like a traditional IRA. Any capital gains or dividends earned by investments in your Roth IRA are not taxed and you can withdraw from your Roth IRA at age 59 ½, tax-free. IRAs are perfectly appropriate investment vehicles for most types of securities, including real estate, exchange-traded funds, mutual funds, certificates of deposit, bonds, and individual stocks. IRAs are also appropriate to hold regular dividend stocks, real-estate investment trusts, royalty trusts and business-development companies. MLPs are an exception and should not be held in an IRA because they lose their tax benefits when held inside an IRA. You should also not hold collectibles in an IRA, including coins, stamps, gems, antiques, and artwork. You cannot buy securities on margin inside of an IRA and cannot hold life insurance policies in an IRA.

Invest in Dividend Stocks with Employer-Sponsored Retirement Accounts

Once you have maxed out your IRAs, you will then want to move on to any retirement plans you have through your employers such as 403Bs and 401Ks. If you are self-employed, you can set up your own retirement plan through individual 401 (K) or through a simplified employee pension. Unfortunately, most employer-sponsored retirement accounts do not permit you to invest in single stocks and give you a limited selection of mutual funds to choose from. Some 401K plans do permit you to place the majority of your 401K contribution into a self-directed brokerage account.

Using health savings account for dividend investing

One additional tax-advantaged investment account that you may not have considered is a health savings account. While most people use HSAs to pay for medical expenses with pre-tax money. HSAs can also be used as a tax-advantaged vehicle to set aside money for the future. If you have a qualifying high-deductible health plan, you can currently set aside $6,500 per year inside of a HAS. With your HAS, you will receive an immediate tax deduction for any contributions you make into a HAS. You can then invest your HSA in mutual funds and have a medical IRA of sorts to pay for future medical expenses or you can use your HSA balance to pay for medical expenses tax-free. You can withdraw the money from your account and pay your ordinary tax rate as you would on a 401K plan or a traditional IRA once you hit age 65.

Traditional Brokerage Account

After you have exhausted all your tax-advantaged investment accounts, you can start investing in dividend stocks through a standard taxable brokerage account. There are many good online discount brokerages that you can use to hold your dividend stock portfolio. Things, you should consider when choosing brokerage account are: the fee you are paying, the research tools that you have access to, website and the brokerage company's track record of customer service. Your best bet is to read the marketing material published by each brokerage and use the brokerage that best suits your need.

ASSET LOCATION MATTERS

If you have different types of investments interspersed between a 401K plan, an IRA and a taxable brokerage account make sure to put your investments that receive the poorest tax treatment inside your tax-advantaged accounts in order to minimize your tax burden. You should put assets that are taxed as ordinary income, such as BDCs, REITs, corporate bonds and some preferred stocks inside your 401k, IRA or other tax-advantaged accounts whenever possible.

Wrap-up

Taxes are dramatically altered by how much of your investment income you actually get to keep. If you were in the top tax bracket, the difference between a tax-free municipal bond and a real-estate investment trust would be 43.4% (3.8% net investment income tax and 39.6% in ordinary income taxes).

Chapter Seven
Building Your Portfolio

N ow you have an understanding on how dividend stocks work, how to evaluate individual dividend stocks, why they are attractive investments, what tools you can use to research dividend stocks and the tax implications of owning different types of dividend stocks. Now we will know how to create a portfolio of dividend stocks and live during retirement off of the income your portfolio generates up to and during retirement.

How your portfolio should look like

Over time, you should work to build a diversified portfolio of 15 to 25 dividend stocks in different industries. A good mix can be some preferred stock or fund, a couple of real-estate investment trusts, a master limited partnership, and several blue-chip stocks.

Your portfolio should target a blended dividend yield of 4% to 5% in order to generate attractive dividend payments without taking on excessive risk. Your portfolio's beta should be around 0.8 if you own a typical mix of dividend stocks. Meaning that it is only 80% as volatile as the broader market indexes. You should target a 10% total annual return between capital gains and the dividend payments you receive. Your portfolio dividend payments should grow by an average of 5% to 8% each year so that the amount of income your portfolio generates increases every year.

Should you include other investments in your income portfolio?

Ultimately, what we are trying to accomplish by buying dividend growth stocks is to create an income stream that we can live off of during retirement. Dividend stocks are popular income generating investment because they offer both near-term income and long-term capital gains. In order to create diversification among the asset classes you own, you may also consider buying municipal bonds if you are in a high tax bracket, buying a rental house or a duplex depending on what your local real estate market looks like or loaning money to other people through peer-to-peer lending websites like Lending Club and Prosper.

Should you simply buy dividend mutual fund?

It can be a lot of work to research individual companies and build a portfolio of 15 to 25 dividend stocks and you may be tempted to just buy a dividend growth mutual fund instead. There are some downsides of buying a mutual fund. First, dividend mutual funds tend to have unimpressive yields. Mutual funds have to own a large number of companies in order to remain fully invested in the market.

Dividend mutual funds and ETFs tend to have relatively high expense ratios relative to the low-cost index funds that are now available. Also, expense ratios eat away at the dividend income you receive.

When you invest in a dividend mutual fund or ETF, you have no control over what companies are included in your portfolio and which are not. You are stuck with the basket of stocks selected by the fund's managers or by the index that the fund tracks. The main reason you might be owning a dividend mutual fund or ETF is diversification. The only scenario where you might consider choosing a divided mutual fund is if you aren't interested or willing to do the research to select individual dividend stocks yourself and want a much more hands-off approach.

Reinvesting your dividends

Many brokers offer dividend reinvestment programs, which allow you to automatically purchase additional shares of a stock with dividend payments that you receive without having to pay a trade fee. It is generally recommended that you reinvest your dividends because your money is immediately put back to work to generate additional dividend income and capital gains. The only other time you might not want to reinvest your dividends when a stock is particularly overvalued and is no longer attractive for additional purchases. In this case, take your dividend payment as cash and reinvest the funds into a dividend stock that is more attractive at the time.

Selling dividend stock

Dividend-growth investing is a long-term play and is very much a buy and hold strategy. As long as your stocks remain attractive and continue to grow their dividend, you should hold on to them. You should cut bait and move the money into a more attractive stock if a company's dividend gets cut and if there is a very strong possibility of it being cut. You can determine when a dividend payment becomes unsustainable by regularly tracking your companies dividend payout ratio. If any of your stocks DPR rises above 905 you should closely monitor them and do additional research to determine if the company's dividend is likely to get cut. You might also consider selling a stock if you can trade it for a better alternative that offers better growth prospects, better yield, and a more sustainable dividend.

Planning your retirement income stream

You should calculate how much income your portfolio of dividend stocks will generate each year by multiplying your portfolio value by its blended dividend yield. Also, calculate any additional income that you have from other investments, such as a 401K plan or rental real-estate. If these are not enough, then you may consider taking a low-stress part-time job to fill the gap.

Once you have taken stock of the various income sources available to you in retirement, you then need to identify which sources you will want to withdraw from first. Generally, you should avoid taking money out of retirement accounts until you need the money or are required to take minimum distributions from a retirement account.

Living off dividend payments

When it becomes time to start relying on your dividend investments to pay for your living expenses during your retirement years, you simply need to stop reinvesting your dividend payments and let them collect in your brokerage account.

Remember that you will owe tax on any dividend payments that you receive from companies held in a taxable brokerage account. In order to minimize any burden from capital gains tax, try to avoid selling any appreciated stocks in your portfolio if at all possible.

The next step is to start taking action. Open a brokerage account with a discount brokerage firm if you don't already have one. Make a small deposit and purchase your first shares of a dividend-paying stock to see how the progress works. If you were to buy 100 shares of a company today that pays a 4% dividend and that dividend grows by 8% each year at the cost of $10000, you would have an income stream of $1, 184, 05 after 10 years if you reinvest your dividends and pay a 15% capital-gains rate.

Chapter Eight
Best Dividend Stocks to Choose

Let's discuss best dividend stocks to invest.

- Johnson & Johnson (JNJ): with a 54-year streak of raising its dividend attests, this 132-year-old healthcare and consumer conglomerate company is a solid choice.
- Store Capital Corp (STOR): boasting a 4.8% dividend, real estate investment trust, Store Capital yields about double what JNJ stock does.
- JPMorgan Chase & Co. (JPM): everyone has heard about JPMorgan. This is a tried-and-true bank that gives investors certain dividend when interest rates rise.
- Amgen (AMGN): currently, Amgen is given 2.6% dividend, but its sustainability is its best feature.
- Oasis Midstream Partners (OMP): Oasis provides midstream services like storing oil and natural gas, gathering and transporting. This company is the smallest, which provides a higher risk/reward for the investors.
- Verizon Communications (VZ): VZ is one of the best dividend stocks to buy. The company operates in the wireless business, which can be slow growing, but it will likely fluctuate less if the market drops.
- Intel Corp (INTC): world famous Intel is certainly a bet. A 36% payout and a 2.5% dividend show that Intel Corp is a trusted investment opportunity.
- Procter & Gamble: this Company survived every American economic fluctuation since 1837. Currently paying a

dividend of 3%, this company is also a solid investment opportunity.

- Starbucks: world famous Starbucks giving dividend yield at 2.1%. Starbucks can be a sound investment for you.
- Mondelez International: this company is a global snacks giant that sells include Cadbury, Nabisco Oreo, Toblerone, Triscuit over 160 companies.
- Colgate-Palmolive: this company is a safe bet for investors who do not want to take any risk.

SOME OTHERS

- Wells Fargo & Co (WFC)
- Exxon Mobile Corporation (XOM)
- Duke Energy Corp (DUK)
- AT&T Inc. (T)
- Welltower Inc (HCN)
- Blackstone Group LP (BX)
- Kimco Reality Corp (KIM)
- Sotherly Hotels Inc (SOHO)
- Abbott Laboratories
- McDonald's
- Chevron Corporation (CVX)
- Medtronic (MDT)
- Stanley Black & Becker (SWK)

Here are some other promising dividend stocks

- Macy's Inc. (M)
- Hersha Hospitality Trust (HT)
- Seagate Technology PLC (STX)

- Consolidated Communications Holdings Inc. (CNSL)
- Washington Prime Group Inc. (WPG)

Chapter Nine
Helpful Resources

The purpose of this book is to provide a solid understanding for anyone who wants to learn about dividend investing. However, beside this book you can research other books on dividend investing, try out various dividend-research tools, and purchase many dividend newsletters. The following contains some books, resources, tools and newsletters that can be helpful in researching dividend stocks.

Books

- Dividends Still Don't Lie by Kelly Wright
- The Single Best Investment by Lowell Miller
- Income Investing Secrets by Richard Stooker
- Get Rich with Dividends by Marc Lichtenfeld
- The Ultimate Dividend Playbook by Josh Peters
- Smart Investors Keep it Simple by Giovanni Rigters
- Dividend Growth Machine by Nathan Winklepleck
- The Great American Dividend Machine by Bill Spetrino
- The Snowball Effect by Timothy J McIntosh
- How to make money is stocks by William J. O'Neil
- One UP On Wall Street by Peter Lynch
- The Ultimate Dividend Playback by Josh Peters

Websites

- www.dividend.com[1]
- www.dividendchannel.com[2]
- www.dividendmonk.com[3]
- www.dripinvesting.org[4]
- www.investopedia.com[5]
- www.marketbeat.com[6]
- www.suredividend.com[7]
- www.seekingalpha.com[8]

Newsletters

- http://mdi.morningstar.com
- http://www.suredividend.com

1. http://www.dividend.com

2. http://www.dividendchannel.com

3. http://www.dividendmonk.com

4. http://www.dripinvesting.org

5. http://www.investopedia.com

6. http://www.marketbeat.com

7. http://www.suredividend.com

8. http://www.seekingalpha.com

Chapter Ten
S&P 500 Index and S&P 500 Dividend Aristocrats

S&P 500 INDEX 2018

Symbol	Name	Price	Dividend Yield (Forward)	PE Ratio (Forward)	Price to Book Value	Market Cap	Beta (3Y)	Return on Equity (TTM)
A	Agilent Technologies	$ 72	0.8%	27.8	4.8	$ 23,170	1.59	15.3%
AAL	American Airlines Group	$ 58	0.7%	11.0	7.1	$ 27,978	1.25	50.5%
AAP	Advance Auto Parts	$ 116	0.2%	16.8	2.7	$ 8,568	0.63	11.7%
AAPL	Apple	$ 177	1.4%	15.4	6.7	$ 900,867	1.32	36.6%
ABBV	AbbVie	$ 100	2.8%	15.1	24.0	$ 160,186	1.40	115.4%
ABC	AmerisourceBergen	$ 99	1.5%	16.3	10.5	$ 21,590	0.98	16.0%
ABT	Abbott Laboratories	$ 59	1.9%	20.8	3.2	$ 102,417	1.65	7.7%
ACN	Accenture	$ 160	1.7%	24.0	11.2	$ 101,923	1.13	42.8%
ADBE	Adobe Systems	$ 195	#N/A	35.1	11.3	$ 95,821	0.94	21.5%
ADI	Analog Devices	$ 92	2.0%	17.7	3.3	$ 33,922	1.30	9.0%
ADM	Archer-Daniels Midland	$ 41	3.2%	15.0	1.3	$ 22,650	1.04	7.1%
ADP	Automatic Data Processing	$ 118	2.1%	30.1	13.3	$ 52,540	0.83	43.9%
ADS	Alliance Data	$ 276	0.8%	12.4	9.6	$	1.58	33.7%

	Systems					15,269		
ADSK	Autodesk	$ 116	#N/A	#N/A	237.9	$ 25,531	2.34	-104.0%
AEE	Ameren	$ 56	3.3%	18.4	1.8	$ 13,471	0.20	8.6%
AEP	American Electric Power	$ 67	3.7%	17.3	1.8	$ 33,182	0.01	10.7%
AES	AES	$ 11	4.7%	9.3	2.3	$ 7,291	1.45	-25.8%
AET	Aetna	$ 184	1.1%	17.5	3.9	$ 60,081	0.55	11.0%
AFL	Aflac	$ 85	2.1%	11.5	1.5	$ 33,394	1.06	12.9%
AGN	Allergan	$ 176	1.6%	11.4	0.9	$ 58,551	1.11	-10.0%
AIG	American International Gr	$ 61	2.1%	11.2	0.8	$ 54,810	1.28	-3.2%
AIV	Apartment Inv & Mgmt	$ 41	3.6%	90.3	4.8	$ 6,378	0.61	14.4%
AIZ	Assurant	$ 95	2.4%	12.8	1.2	$ 5,133	0.57	5.6%
AJG	Arthur J. Gallagher	$ 64	2.4%	18.7	2.8	$ 11,549	1.31	12.0%
AKAM	Akamai Technologies	$ 66	#N/A	24.6	3.4	$ 11,083	0.35	9.0%
ALB	Albemarle	$ 134	1.0%	26.0	3.8	$ 14,753	2.30	23.8%
ALGN	Align Technology	$ 258	#N/A	58.3	17.5	$ 20,720	1.62	25.5%
ALK	Alaska Air Group	$ 74	1.6%	11.2	2.6	$ 9,046	0.38	24.9%
ALL	Allstate	$ 102	1.5%	12.0	1.8	$	1.02	14.2%

						36,640		
ALLE	Allegion	$ 85	0.8%	20.1	22.0	$ 8,082	1.14	161.3%
ALXN	Alexion Pharmaceuticals	$ 123	#N/A	17.3	3.1	$ 27,415	1.05	5.8%
AMAT	Applied Materials	$ 53	0.8%	13.3	6.0	$ 56,461	1.72	41.7%
AMD	Advanced Micro Devices	$ 12	#N/A	33.6	22.3	$ 11,597	2.98	-16.1%
AME	AMETEK	$ 75	0.5%	26.1	4.6	$ 17,380	1.19	15.9%
AMG	Affiliated Managers Group	$ 203	0.4%	11.6	3.1	$ 11,272	1.86	14.9%
AMGN	Amgen	$ 185	2.9%	14.5	4.2	$ 134,322	1.70	26.3%
AMP	Ameriprise Financial	$ 182	1.8%	13.4	4.3	$ 26,929	2.08	26.7%
AMT	American Tower	$ 133	2.1%	36.1	8.6	$ 56,253	0.89	18.4%
AMZN	Amazon.com	$ 1,305	#N/A	161.4	25.5	$ 628,940	1.33	9.0%
ANDV	Andeavor	$ 119	2.0%	12.8	2.0	$ 18,584	1.10	10.6%
ANSS	Ansys	$ 154	#N/A	36.5	5.7	$ 13,087	1.03	12.4%
ANTM	Anthem	$ 240	1.2%	18.2	2.4	$ 61,576	0.77	11.6%
AON	Aon	$ 137	1.1%	17.1	6.6	$ 34,124	1.01	31.1%
AOS	A.O. Smith	$ 65	0.9%	26.9	6.7	$	1.31	22.6%

						11,230		
APA	Apache	$ 47	2.1%	56.7	2.6	$ 17,965	1.52	10.1%
APC	Anadarko Petroleum	$ 59	0.3%	#N/A	3.0	$ 32,271	1.89	-16.5%
APD	Air Products & Chemicals	$ 170	2.2%	24.2	3.7	$ 37,232	1.07	34.8%
APH	Amphenol	$ 92	0.8%	26.6	6.9	$ 28,039	0.82	26.0%
APTV	Aptiv	$ 93	1.0%	17.9	7.7	$ 24,699	1.64	50.6%
ARE	Alexandria Real Estate	$ 125	2.9%	59.0	2.2	$ 11,976	1.04	3.1%
ARNC	Arconic	$ 31	0.8%	19.9	2.5	$ 14,844	#N/A	-11.0%
ATVI	Activision Blizzard	$ 70	0.4%	27.6	5.3	$ 53,199	0.57	11.8%
AVB	AvalonBay Communities	$ 168	3.4%	35.4	2.2	$ 23,231	0.40	8.6%
AVGO	Broadcom	$ 264	2.7%	13.5	5.1	$ 103,311	1.02	8.7%
AVY	Avery Dennison	$ 119	1.5%	21.6	9.3	$ 10,507	1.25	38.9%
AWK	American Water Works Co	$ 81	2.1%	24.6	2.6	$ 14,418	0.04	9.9%
AXP	American Express	$ 101	1.4%	13.9	4.2	$ 87,642	1.16	22.7%
AYI	Acuity Brands	$ 159	0.3%	16.8	3.9	$ 6,692	1.42	18.4%
AZO	AutoZone	$ 788	#N/A	16.3	#N/	$	0.60	-76.5%

							A	21,552		
BA	Boeing	$ 336	2.0%	29.0	184.4	$ 200,239			1.28	1633.2%
BAC	Bank of America	$ 31	1.5%	12.8	1.3	$ 325,331			1.78	8.3%
BAX	Baxter International	$ 68	0.9%	25.1	3.9	$ 37,234			0.84	11.6%
BBT	BB&T	$ 53	2.5%	13.8	1.6	$ 41,923			1.18	8.8%
BBY	Best Buy Co	$ 73	1.9%	18.2	5.2	$ 21,413			0.33	28.3%
BDX	Becton, Dickinson and Co	$ 228	1.3%	21.0	4.0	$ 52,238			0.96	11.3%
BEN	Franklin Resources	$ 45	2.1%	14.4	2.0	$ 24,621			1.60	13.9%
BF.B	Brown-Forman	$ 66	1.2%	33.3	15.4	$ 25,386			0.74	53.9%
BHF	Brighthouse Financial	$ 65	#N/A	6.8	0.6	$ 7,828		#N/A		-18.7%
BHGE	Baker Hughes, a GE	$ 37	1.9%	34.7	2.8	$ 42,605			0.42	#N/A
BIIB	Biogen	$ 336	#N/A	14.0	5.5	$ 71,046			0.59	29.0%
BK	Bank of New York Mellon	$ 58	1.6%	13.9	1.6	$ 59,823			1.19	10.4%
BLK	BlackRock	$ 556	2.1%	19.5	3.0	$ 89,069			1.73	12.0%
BLL	Ball	$ 38	1.1%	16.7	3.8	$ 13,267			0.92	7.5%

BMY	Bristol-Myers Squibb	$ 63	2.6%	19.6	7.0	$ 102,801	1.01	27.9%
BRK.B	Berkshire Hathaway	$ 210	#N/A	24.3	1.7	$ 518,503	0.79	6.4%
BSX	Boston Scientific	$ 27	#N/A	19.9	5.0	$ 37,708	0.81	12.0%
BWA	BorgWarner	$ 57	1.2%	13.7	3.2	$ 12,066	1.95	8.2%
BXP	Boston Properties	$ 122	2.6%	42.3	3.4	$ 18,878	0.92	9.1%
C	Citigroup	$ 77	1.7%	12.4	1.0	$ 203,165	1.68	7.5%
CA	CA	$ 34	3.0%	13.9	2.4	$ 14,268	0.59	12.7%
CAG	Conagra Brands	$ 37	2.3%	19.3	4.0	$ 14,708	0.24	17.5%
CAH	Cardinal Health	$ 71	2.6%	14.0	3.4	$ 22,491	0.88	16.6%
CAT	Caterpillar	$ 170	1.8%	21.1	6.5	$ 101,317	1.61	6.1%
CB	Chubb	$ 146	2.0%	13.5	1.3	$ 67,609	0.82	8.0%
CBG	CBRE Group	$ 45	#N/A	15.9	4.0	$ 15,238	2.29	23.9%
CBOE	Cboe Global Markets	$ 132	0.8%	29.2	5.2	$ 14,921	0.27	10.4%
CBS	CBS	$ 59	1.2%	11.7	7.5	$ 22,492	1.38	8.1%
CCI	Crown Castle Intl	$ 104	4.1%	81.9	3.3	$ 42,078	0.17	5.6%

CCL	Carnival	$ 70	2.6%	16.4	2.1	$ 50,037	0.84 11.2%
CDNS	Cadence Design Systems	$ 45	#N/A	29.6	12.6	$ 12,726	1.02 28.7%
CELG	Celgene	$ 106	#N/A	12.0	8.5	$ 83,456	1.22 44.8%
CERN	Cerner	$ 73	#N/A	27.6	5.3	$ 24,233	0.89 16.0%
CF	CF Industries Holdings	$ 44	2.8%	91.4	3.2	$ 10,151	1.16 -12.6%
CFG	Citizens Financial Group	$ 46	1.6%	14.5	1.1	$ 22,395	1.38 6.4%
CHD	Church & Dwight Co	$ 49	1.6%	23.0	6.3	$ 12,251	0.27 22.8%
CHK	Chesapeake Energy	$ 4	#N/A	5.4	#N/A	$ 3,889	2.41 -8.7%
CHRW	C.H. Robinson Worldwide	$ 94	2.0%	22.8	9.7	$ 13,171	0.65 36.3%
CHTR	Charter Communications	$ 354	#N/A	62.7	2.7	$ 88,455	1.36 2.1%
CI	Cigna	$ 213	0.0%	17.8	3.7	$ 52,611	0.40 16.7%
CINF	Cincinnati Financial	$ 74	2.7%	23.6	1.6	$ 12,146	0.79 6.9%
CL	Colgate-Palmolive	$ 75	2.1%	24.1	#N/A	$ 65,524	0.68 -1110.2%
CLX	Clorox	$ 141	2.4%	24.9	30.7	$ 18,175	0.26 170.2%
CMA	Comerica	$ 93	1.3%	15.2	2.0	$ 16,181	1.72 10.0%

CMCSA	Comcast	$ 42	1.5%	18.3	3.6	$ 198,355	1.23	18.4%
CME	CME Group	$ 153	1.7%	25.9	2.5	$ 51,973	0.89	7.2%
CMG	Chipotle Mexican Grill	$ 327	#N/A	33.9	6.7	$ 9,242	0.19	10.5%
CMI	Cummins	$ 184	2.4%	15.7	4.0	$ 30,568	0.80	22.9%
CMS	CMS Energy	$ 44	3.0%	18.9	2.7	$ 12,395	-0.06	12.3%
CNC	Centene	$ 109	#N/A	18.4	2.8	$ 18,893	0.93	14.0%
CNP	CenterPoint Energy	$ 27	4.1%	18.9	3.3	$ 11,797	0.53	16.9%
COF	Capital One Financial	$ 105	1.5%	11.3	1.0	$ 51,107	1.32	7.7%
COG	Cabot Oil & Gas	$ 29	0.8%	29.5	5.1	$ 13,357	0.76	-5.5%
COL	Rockwell Collins	$ 138	1.0%	19.4	3.7	$ 22,566	0.65	19.2%
COO	The Cooper Companies	$ 231	0.0%	20.1	3.6	$ 11,299	0.76	12.7%
COP	ConocoPhillips	$ 60	1.8%	36.6	2.4	$ 71,791	1.49	-7.4%
COST	Costco Wholesale	$ 192	1.0%	28.9	7.6	$ 84,238	1.07	24.7%
COTY	Coty	$ 21	2.4%	30.4	1.6	$ 15,574	0.08	-5.8%
CPB	Campbell Soup	$ 46	3.1%	15.4	8.1	$ 13,681	-0.05	55.4%

CRM	Salesforce.com	$ 110	#N/A	82.6	9.0	$ 79,626	1.56	0.1%
CSCO	Cisco Systems	$ 41	2.8%	16.6	3.1	$ 202,046	1.53	14.9%
CSRA	CSRA	$ 32	1.3%	16.2	11.8	$ 5,254	#N/A	96.6%
CSX	CSX	$ 59	1.4%	19.9	4.9	$ 52,953	1.33	15.6%
CTAS	Cintas	$ 160	1.0%	27.9	6.7	$ 17,087	0.96	23.9%
CTL	CenturyLink	$ 17	12.4%	12.3	1.4	$ 18,558	0.72	2.4%
CTSH	Cognizant Tech Solns	$ 75	0.8%	17.1	4.0	$ 43,964	0.98	18.5%
CTXS	Citrix Systems	$ 90	#N/A	18.6	6.8	$ 13,567	1.56	21.9%
CVS	CVS Health	$ 79	2.5%	12.1	2.3	$ 79,811	0.56	14.4%
CVX	Chevron	$ 134	3.2%	23.6	1.7	$ 253,756	1.32	4.4%
CXO	Concho Resources	$ 159	#N/A	62.8	2.7	$ 23,656	1.02	6.9%
D	Dominion Energy	$ 76	4.1%	18.8	3.0	$ 48,870	0.20	14.2%
DAL	Delta Air Lines	$ 60	2.0%	9.6	3.1	$ 42,657	0.88	27.8%
DE	Deere	$ 169	1.4%	20.5	5.7	$ 54,615	0.86	27.4%
DFS	Discover Financial	$ 81	1.7%	11.0	2.8	$ 29,256	1.73	21.2%

AUTOMATIC PASSIVE INCOME - HOW THE BEST DIVIDEND STOCKS CAN GENERATE PASSIVE INCOME FOR WEALTH BUILDING.

63

DG	Dollar General	$ 99	1.1%	21.8	4.7	$ 26,912	0.66	22.4%
DGX	Quest Diagnostics	$ 102	1.8%	17.2	2.9	$ 13,852	0.94	14.4%
DHI	D.R. Horton	$ 52	1.0%	14.0	2.5	$ 19,518	1.11	14.4%
DHR	Danaher	$ 99	0.6%	22.9	2.7	$ 69,136	1.02	9.9%
DIS	Walt Disney	$ 112	1.5%	17.6	4.1	$ 169,524	1.35	21.0%
DISCA	Discovery Communications	$ 24	#N/A	10.8	1.6	$ 9,222	1.65	20.6%
DISCK	Discovery Communications	$ 23	#N/A	10.2	1.5	$ 8,718	1.43	20.6%
DISH	DISH Network	$ 49	#N/A	23.0	4.2	$ 23,075	0.95	20.5%
DLR	Digital Realty Trust	$ 106	3.5%	62.2	2.4	$ 21,732	0.14	5.3%
DLTR	Dollar Tree Stores	$ 115	#N/A	23.5	4.5	$ 27,228	0.58	17.8%
DOV	Dover	$ 104	1.8%	22.8	3.8	$ 16,224	1.22	17.0%
DPS	Dr Pepper Snapple Group	$ 95	2.4%	18.4	8.1	$ 17,195	0.42	34.1%
DRE	Duke Realty	$ 26	3.1%	57.4	1.9	$ 9,156	0.71	37.8%
DRI	Darden Restaurants	$ 98	2.6%	20.6	6.1	$ 12,109	-0.13	24.7%
DTE	DTE Energy	$ 104	3.4%	18.2	2.0	$ 18,642	0.02	10.7%

DUK	Duke Energy	$ 79	4.5%	16.4	1.3	$ 55,228	0.02	5.2%
DVA	DaVita	$ 79	#N/A	20.8	3.0	$ 14,505	1.07	10.5%
DVN	Devon Energy	$ 44	0.5%	17.5	3.2	$ 23,143	2.72	24.0%
DWDP	DowDuPont	$ 75	2.0%	18.6	1.7	$ 176,459	1.48	6.6%
DXC	DXC Technology	$ 101	0.7%	13.4	2.4	$ 28,895	#N/A	5.0%
EA	Electronic Arts	$ 113	#N/A	26.8	7.9	$ 34,836	0.45	29.5%
EBAY	eBay	$ 38	#N/A	17.1	3.5	$ 39,715	1.71	72.7%
ECL	Ecolab	$ 138	1.2%	26.1	5.5	$ 39,778	1.07	18.8%
ED	Consolidated Edison	$ 79	3.5%	18.7	1.6	$ 24,647	-0.13	9.3%
EFX	Equifax	$ 123	1.3%	20.6	4.8	$ 14,752	0.92	18.7%
EIX	Edison International	$ 61	3.9%	14.4	1.6	$ 20,011	-0.13	12.9%
EL	The Estee Lauder	$ 129	1.2%	30.7	10.0	$ 47,330	0.74	33.4%
EMN	Eastman Chemical	$ 97	2.3%	11.9	2.8	$ 14,004	1.20	21.5%
EMR	Emerson Electric	$ 74	2.6%	25.3	5.4	$ 47,202	1.28	19.0%
EOG	EOG Resources	$ 116	0.6%	55.7	4.8	$ 66,900	1.08	0.1%

EQIX	Equinix	$ 436	1.8%	68.8	5.2	$ 34,106	0.66	4.0%
EQR	Equity Residential	$ 60	3.3%	42.3	2.2	$ 22,203	0.49	7.4%
EQT	EQT	$ 58	0.2%	37.5	2.5	$ 15,506	0.56	0.6%
ES	Eversource Energy	$ 61	3.1%	18.5	1.8	$ 19,441	0.07	9.1%
ESRX	Express Scripts Holding	$ 81	#N/A	9.4	2.9	$ 45,803	1.00	22.8%
ESS	Essex Property Trust	$ 227	3.1%	47.8	2.4	$ 14,997	0.46	8.4%
ETFC	E*TRADE Financial	$ 54	#N/A	17.1	2.3	$ 14,456	1.45	10.1%
ETN	Eaton	$ 84	2.9%	16.6	2.2	$ 37,116	1.36	18.4%
ETR	Entergy	$ 78	4.6%	15.5	1.6	$ 14,099	0.50	-10.0%
EVHC	Envision Healthcare	$ 36	#N/A	10.9	0.7	$ 4,322	-0.08	-8.9%
EW	Edwards Lifesciences	$ 121	#N/A	28.5	8.1	$ 25,570	0.69	26.3%
EXC	Exelon	$ 38	3.4%	13.1	1.3	$ 36,887	0.27	7.8%
EXPD	Expeditors International	$ 67	1.3%	24.4	6.0	$ 11,858	0.71	22.6%
EXPE	Expedia	$ 132	0.9%	24.4	4.4	$ 20,184	0.90	9.6%
EXR	Extra Space Storage	$ 82	3.8%	27.7	4.7	$ 10,364	0.36	15.5%

F	Ford Motor	$ 13	4.5%	8.3	1.6	$ 52,554	1.30 14.1%
FAST	Fastenal	$ 56	2.3%	25.8	7.9	$ 15,976	0.89 27.5%
FB	Facebook	$ 179	#N/A	26.7	7.3	$ 521,215	0.56 24.3%
FBHS	Fortune Brands Home	$ 71	1.1%	20.2	4.2	$ 10,720	1.09 18.3%
FCX	Freeport-McMoRan	$ 20	#N/A	11.3	4.1	$ 28,590	3.30 14.2%
FDX	FedEx	$ 272	0.7%	20.2	4.3	$ 72,826	1.52 18.6%
FE	FirstEnergy	$ 30	4.8%	11.8	2.1	$ 13,377	0.09 -68.6%
FFIV	F5 Networks	$ 142	#N/A	16.3	7.2	$ 8,876	1.00 35.1%
FIS	Fidelity National Info	$ 98	1.2%	20.0	3.3	$ 32,589	0.88 5.5%
FISV	Fiserv	$ 137	#N/A	23.9	12.2	$ 28,597	0.79 37.3%
FITB	Fifth Third Bancorp	$ 32	2.0%	14.3	1.5	$ 22,826	1.57 13.8%
FL	Foot Locker	$ 47	2.6%	11.6	2.2	$ 5,751	0.37 19.0%
FLIR	FLIR Systems	$ 50	1.2%	23.7	3.7	$ 6,968	0.65 12.6%
FLR	Fluor	$ 57	1.5%	23.8	2.4	$ 7,983	1.49 6.3%
FLS	Flowserve	$ 44	1.7%	23.8	3.3	$ 5,748	1.47 10.0%
FMC	FMC	$ 98	0.7%	18.7	6.2	$ 13,142	1.92 1.1%
FOX	Twenty-First Century Fox	$ 36	1.0%	18.1	4.1	$ 67,377	1.43 19.9%

AUTOMATIC PASSIVE INCOME - HOW THE BEST DIVIDEND STOCKS CAN GENERATE PASSIVE INCOME FOR WEALTH BUILDING.

67

FOXA	Twenty-First Century Fox	$ 37	1.0%	18.3	4.2	$ 68,043	1.43	19.9%
FRT	Federal Realty Investment	$ 123	3.3%	39.2	4.3	$ 8,909	0.29	15.0%
FTI	TechnipFMC	$ 35	1.5%	#N/A	1.2	$ 16,197	1.12	5.5%
FTV	Fortive	$ 74	0.4%	23.1	7.5	$ 25,883	#N/A	31.5%
GD	General Dynamics	$ 211	1.6%	19.3	5.4	$ 62,879	0.79	29.1%
GE	General Electric	$ 19	2.6%	18.2	2.1	$ 162,688	0.90	9.8%
GGP	GGP	$ 23	3.8%	34.8	2.8	$ 22,186	0.79	8.3%
GILD	Gilead Sciences	$ 79	2.6%	11.7	4.2	$ 103,221	0.85	55.9%
GIS	General Mills	$ 58	3.4%	18.5	7.8	$ 32,919	0.49	38.7%
GLW	Corning	$ 35	1.8%	19.3	2.0	$ 29,940	1.11	16.0%
GM	General Motors	$ 44	3.5%	7.4	1.5	$ 62,597	1.66	7.0%
GOOG	Alphabet	$ 1,122	#N/A	26.7	5.0	$ 779,749	1.06	14.5%
GOOGL	Alphabet	$ 1,131	#N/A	26.9	5.0	$ 785,578	1.02	14.5%
GPC	Genuine Parts	$ 103	2.6%	17.8	4.5	$ 15,142	1.07	20.2%
GPN	Global Payments	$ 103	0.0%	21.8	4.7	$ 16,433	1.03	9.5%

GPS	Gap	$ 34	2.7%	16.1	4.4	$ 13,171	0.60	29.8%
GRMN	Garmin	$ 62	3.3%	20.9	3.2	$ 11,630	0.74	19.7%
GS	Goldman Sachs Group	$ 257	1.2%	12.3	1.3	$ 96,952	1.51	11.3%
GT	Goodyear Tire & Rubber	$ 34	1.7%	9.0	1.7	$ 8,353	1.57	21.3%
GWW	W.W. Grainger	$ 236	2.2%	21.0	7.6	$ 13,429	0.62	27.1%
HAL	Halliburton	$ 53	1.4%	24.0	5.0	$ 46,367	1.12	2.3%
HAS	Hasbro	$ 92	2.5%	17.7	5.9	$ 11,515	0.59	32.2%
HBAN	Huntington Bancshares	$ 16	2.8%	13.4	1.8	$ 17,133	1.46	10.5%
HBI	Hanesbrands	$ 22	2.7%	10.8	6.6	$ 8,174	0.17	53.2%
HCA	HCA Healthcare	$ 89	#N/A	11.9	#N/A	$ 31,440	0.22	-37.3%
HCN	Welltower	$ 59	5.9%	30.4	1.6	$ 21,910	0.24	7.0%
HCP	HCP	$ 24	6.3%	29.8	2.0	$ 11,090	0.43	8.4%
HD	Home Depot	$ 196	1.8%	26.5	90.2	$ 229,369	1.03	214.7%
HES	Hess	$ 55	1.8%	#N/A	1.3	$ 17,330	1.80	-41.7%
HIG	Hartford Financial	$ 55	1.8%	12.8	1.1	$ 19,723	0.71	2.8%

HII	Huntington Ingalls Indus	$ 247	1.2%	18.4	6.5	$ 11,199	1.34	36.8%
HLT	Hilton Worldwide Holdings	$ 84	0.7%	34.0	18.6	$ 26,860	1.46	0.9%
HOG	Harley-Davidson	$ 54	2.7%	14.3	4.9	$ 9,157	0.75	28.6%
HOLX	Hologic	$ 44	#N/A	20.0	4.3	$ 12,050	0.60	29.5%
HON	Honeywell International	$ 159	1.9%	20.3	5.7	$ 120,386	1.02	25.4%
HP	Helmerich & Payne	$ 70	4.0%	#N/A	1.8	$ 7,631	1.57	-2.9%
HPE	Hewlett Packard Enterprise	$ 16	1.9%	#N/A	1.1	$ 25,199	#N/A	1.2%
HPQ	HP	$ 23	2.4%	12.7	#N/A	$ 37,709	1.83	-63.4%
HRB	H&R Block	$ 26	3.6%	13.3	#N/A	$ 5,511	-0.28	-96.4%
HRL	Hormel Foods	$ 35	2.2%	20.0	3.7	$ 18,297	0.29	18.1%
HRS	Harris	$ 147	1.6%	23.7	5.9	$ 17,548	1.16	18.4%
HSIC	Henry Schein	$ 75	#N/A	18.9	3.9	$ 11,746	0.87	19.2%
HST	Host Hotels & Resorts	$ 20	3.9%	30.4	2.1	$ 15,068	1.23	8.5%
HSY	The Hershey	$ 109	2.4%	20.9	28.0	$ 23,023	0.06	85.8%
HUM	Humana	$ 268	0.6%	22.1	3.4	$ 38,289	0.63	17.1%
IBM	IBM	$ 163	3.7%	11.8	7.7	$	1.07	61.7%

						151,034		
ICE	Intercontinental Exchange	$ 75	1.1%	21.2	2.7	$ 43,748	0.63	10.4%
IDXX	IDEXX Laboratories	$ 173	#N/A	48.7	#N/A	$ 15,110	0.28	-528.0%
IFF	International Flavors	$ 154	1.8%	24.3	6.9	$ 12,139	1.29	24.8%
ILMN	Illumina	$ 245	#N/A	53.1	12.5	$ 35,729	0.81	31.1%
INCY	Incyte	$ 94	#N/A	187.5	11.3	$ 19,852	1.12	-17.0%
INFO	IHS Markit	$ 48	#N/A	21.7	2.5	$ 19,087	0.81	5.1%
INTC	Intel	$ 43	2.5%	13.3	2.9	$ 202,363	1.23	20.6%
INTU	Intuit	$ 165	1.0%	32.5	35.0	$ 42,057	1.42	82.3%
IP	International Paper	$ 62	3.1%	14.3	5.2	$ 25,709	1.71	20.0%
IPG	The Interpublic Group	$ 22	3.3%	13.8	4.2	$ 8,448	1.43	29.2%
IQV	IQVIA Holdings	$ 100	#N/A	18.8	2.9	$ 20,807	0.58	0.9%
IR	Ingersoll-Rand	$ 91	2.0%	17.5	3.4	$ 22,763	1.24	15.5%
IRM	Iron Mountain	$ 36	6.5%	27.2	5.5	$ 10,194	0.40	10.8%
ISRG	Intuitive Surgical	$ 419	#N/A	44.4	9.5	$ 46,953	0.90	18.1%

IT	Gartner	$ 130	#N/A	32.4	13.7	$ 11,796	0.96 -10.0%
ITW	Illinois Tool Works	$ 171	1.8%	23.6	11.6	$ 58,420	1.22 48.7%
IVZ	Invesco	$ 38	3.1%	12.5	1.9	$ 15,412	1.95 12.1%
JBHT	JB Hunt Transport	$ 121	0.8%	24.2	9.0	$ 13,287	1.24 29.7%
JCI	Johnson Controls	$ 40	2.5%	14.3	1.8	$ 36,832	0.68 7.8%
JEC	Jacobs Engineering Group	$ 70	0.9%	18.5	2.2	$ 9,828	1.68 7.0%
JNJ	Johnson & Johnson	$ 146	2.3%	18.6	5.3	$ 391,587	0.64 22.0%
JNPR	Juniper Networks	$ 29	1.4%	13.6	2.1	$ 10,832	1.47 12.9%
JPM	JPMorgan Chase	$ 113	2.0%	13.0	1.7	$ 390,934	1.34 11.7%
JWN	Nordstrom	$ 52	2.9%	17.5	10.1	$ 8,632	0.74 60.3%
K	Kellogg	$ 65	3.3%	15.1	11.6	$ 22,349	0.16 40.0%
KEY	KeyCorp	$ 21	2.0%	13.0	1.6	$ 23,035	0.94 9.5%
KHC	Kraft Heinz	$ 77	3.2%	19.7	1.6	$ 94,248	#N/A 6.8%
KIM	Kimco Realty	$ 17	6.7%	28.1	1.4	$ 7,134	0.38 8.0%
KLAC	KLA-Tencor	$ 107	2.2%	15.0	11.5	$ 16,813	1.73 90.5%
KMB	Kimberly-Clark	$ 113	3.4%	17.1	153.4	$	0.70 1560.5%

						39,742		
KMI	Kinder Morgan	$ 20	2.6%	26.9	1.2	$ 43,593	0.61	4.0%
KMX	CarMax	$ 72	#N/A	18.7	4.0	$ 13,081	1.50	22.0%
KO	Coca-Cola	$ 46	3.2%	23.0	8.9	$ 196,630	0.55	19.6%
KORS	Michael Kors Holdings	$ 65	#N/A	16.4	5.5	$ 9,922	-0.45	33.7%
KR	Kroger	$ 28	1.8%	13.9	4.0	$ 24,802	0.43	24.5%
KSS	Kohl's	$ 64	3.4%	15.7	2.1	$ 10,730	1.21	12.7%
KSU	Kansas City Southern	$ 110	1.3%	17.2	2.8	$ 11,431	0.74	13.1%
L	Loews	$ 53	0.5%	16.3	0.9	$ 17,767	0.66	5.2%
LB	L Brands	$ 50	4.8%	15.9	#N/A	$ 14,020	0.45	-99.3%
LEG	Leggett & Platt	$ 49	3.0%	17.8	5.5	$ 6,433	0.89	30.4%
LEN	Lennar	$ 69	0.2%	13.1	2.2	$ 16,620	1.31	11.5%
LH	Laboratory Corp	$ 172	#N/A	16.4	2.9	$ 17,473	1.18	13.0%
LKQ	LKQ	$ 43	#N/A	19.7	3.3	$ 13,434	0.99	13.5%
LLL	L3 Technologies	$ 209	1.4%	23.2	3.3	$ 16,368	1.40	12.1%
LLY	Eli Lilly	$ 87	2.6%	18.7	6.4	$	0.10	15.3%

AUTOMATIC PASSIVE INCOME - HOW THE BEST DIVIDEND STOCKS CAN GENERATE PASSIVE INCOME FOR WEALTH BUILDING.

73

95,773

LMT	Lockheed Martin	$ 336	2.4%	24.1	46.0	$ 96,414	0.64	209.2%
LNC	Lincoln National	$ 84	1.6%	10.0	1.1	$ 18,463	2.24	9.3%
LNT	Alliant Energy	$ 40	3.2%	18.7	2.2	$ 9,140	0.23	11.0%
LOW	Lowe's Companies	$ 101	1.6%	22.1	14.6	$ 83,690	1.11	59.6%
LRCX	Lam Research	$ 189	1.1%	12.9	4.2	$ 30,528	1.68	30.3%
LUK	Leucadia National	$ 28	1.4%	17.2	1.0	$ 9,951	1.23	5.6%
LUV	Southwest Airlines	$ 65	0.8%	13.0	4.4	$ 38,784	1.18	25.2%
LYB	LyondellBasell Industries	$ 118	3.1%	12.4	6.3	$ 46,420	1.20	57.2%
M	Macy's	$ 27	5.6%	7.5	1.9	$ 8,190	0.74	16.6%
MA	Mastercard	$ 162	0.6%	30.0	26.7	$ 171,853	1.13	77.6%
MAA	Mid-America Apartment	$ 91	4.0%	27.0	1.6	$ 10,376	0.24	4.3%
MAC	Macerich	$ 63	4.7%	83.8	2.4	$ 8,864	0.71	3.8%
MAR	Marriott International	$ 140	0.9%	27.6	11.3	$ 50,961	1.42	27.4%
MAS	Masco	$ 46	0.9%	19.7	#N/A	$ 14,395	1.48	-285.1%
MAT	Mattel	$ 15	#N/A	39.3	3.7	$ 5,256	0.78	-28.4%
MCD	McDonald's	$ 174	2.3%	24.4	#N/A	$ 138,368	0.79	-250.8%
MCHP	Microchip	$ 93	1.6%	17.2	6.2	$	1.12	19.7%

	Technology					21,856		
MCK	McKesson	$ 166	0.8%	13.6	3.1	$ 34,659	1.30	44.7%
MCO	Moody's	$ 157	1.0%	23.6	#N/A	$ 30,050	1.10	-72.6%
MDLZ	Mondelez International	$ 42	2.1%	18.0	2.4	$ 63,467	0.62	8.5%
MDT	Medtronic	$ 85	2.2%	17.9	2.2	$ 115,656	0.71	10.0%
MET	MetLife	$ 53	3.0%	11.0	1.0	$ 56,119	1.42	-0.7%
MGM	MGM Resorts International	$ 35	1.3%	23.8	3.1	$ 19,832	1.80	9.4%
MHK	Mohawk Industries	$ 274	#N/A	18.4	3.0	$ 20,374	1.24	15.7%
MKC	McCormick & Co	$ 101	2.1%	21.6	5.2	$ 13,232	0.30	24.4%
MLM	Martin Marietta Materials	$ 231	0.8%	26.1	3.3	$ 14,505	1.37	10.4%
MMC	Marsh & McLennan	$ 82	1.8%	19.1	5.9	$ 41,717	1.00	28.4%
MMM	3M	$ 244	1.9%	24.8	12.0	$ 145,608	0.95	48.1%
MNST	Monster Beverage	$ 64	#N/A	35.5	9.5	$ 35,964	0.85	22.3%
MO	Altria Group	$ 70	3.8%	18.9	10.9	$ 132,829	0.43	147.8%
MON	Monsanto	$ 120	1.8%	21.1	8.0	$ 52,771	0.95	40.7%

MOS	Mosaic	$ 27	0.4%	23.5	0.9	$ 9,556	1.58	3.4%
MPC	Marathon Petroleum	$ 71	2.2%	14.0	2.7	$ 34,882	1.70	12.5%
MRK	Merck & Co	$ 59	3.3%	14.4	4.2	$ 159,815	0.85	7.1%
MRO	Marathon Oil	$ 19	1.1%	#N/A	1.4	$ 15,991	3.01	-48.2%
MS	Morgan Stanley	$ 55	1.8%	12.9	1.4	$ 99,651	1.64	10.2%
MSFT	Microsoft	$ 90	1.9%	26.4	7.7	$ 691,227	1.46	31.1%
MSI	Motorola Solutions	$ 97	2.2%	16.4	#N/A	$ 15,644	0.39	-73.8%
MTB	M&T Bank	$ 179	1.7%	16.1	1.8	$ 26,870	0.99	9.4%
MTD	Mettler-Toledo Intl	$ 651	#N/A	32.6	32.4	$ 16,642	1.16	92.9%
MU	Micron Technology	$ 43	#N/A	4.4	2.2	$ 49,502	2.07	45.2%
MYL	Mylan	$ 47	#N/A	8.7	1.9	$ 25,159	1.48	7.2%
NAVI	Navient	$ 14	4.6%	7.4	1.0	$ 3,651	2.41	14.4%
NBL	Noble Energy	$ 32	1.2%	115.5	1.7	$ 15,683	1.03	-19.7%
NCLH	Norwegian Cruise Line	$ 58	#N/A	12.6	2.4	$ 13,217	1.60	15.1%
NDAQ	Nasdaq	$ 81	1.9%	17.1	2.4	$ 13,536	0.70	4.7%
NEE	NextEra Energy	$ 150	2.6%	#N/A	2.7	$	0.15	16.6%

						70,710		
NEM	Newmont Mining	$ 40	0.8%	29.3	1.9	$ 21,221	0.15	0.8%
NFLX	Netflix	$ 221	#N/A	95.3	28.8	$ 95,733	0.66	15.1%
NFX	Newfield Exploration	$ 35	#N/A	12.7	5.3	$ 6,937	1.49	31.6%
NI	NiSource	$ 24	2.9%	18.7	1.9	$ 8,107	0.15	6.6%
NKE	Nike	$ 65	1.2%	28.1	8.9	$ 105,214	0.51	31.6%
NLSN	Nielsen Holdings	$ 37	3.6%	14.3	3.1	$ 13,342	0.79	12.1%
NOC	Northrop Grumman	$ 315	1.3%	23.4	8.4	$ 54,861	0.70	40.7%
NOV	National Oilwell Varco	$ 39	0.5%	113.0	1.1	$ 14,874	0.92	-6.6%
NRG	NRG Energy	$ 29	0.4%	13.2	7.7	$ 9,088	1.47	-90.0%
NSC	Norfolk Southern	$ 154	1.6%	19.3	3.5	$ 44,164	1.56	14.8%
NTAP	NetApp	$ 63	1.3%	18.9	6.0	$ 16,747	1.91	23.4%
NTRS	Northern Trust	$ 107	1.6%	17.8	2.6	$ 24,393	1.11	12.3%
NUE	Nucor	$ 69	2.2%	15.0	2.6	$ 21,943	1.81	13.5%
NVDA	NVIDIA	$ 223	0.3%	50.0	21.3	$ 135,126	1.43	43.7%
NWL	Newell Brands	$ 32	2.9%	10.9	1.2	$ 15,811	1.02	10.6%

NWS	News	$ 18	1.1%	36.8	0.9	$ 10,225	2.08	-5.9%
NWSA	News	$ 17	1.2%	35.9	0.9	$ 9,992	2.27	-5.9%
O	Realty Income	$ 53	4.8%	41.3	2.0	$ 14,856	-0.03	5.1%
OKE	ONEOK	$ 59	5.1%	25.7	4.3	$ 22,801	1.15	18.2%
OMC	Omnicom Group	$ 76	3.2%	13.9	6.9	$ 17,502	1.20	51.9%
ORCL	Oracle	$ 50	1.5%	16.8	3.7	$ 204,952	1.03	18.7%
ORLY	O'Reilly Automotive	$ 259	#N/A	19.0	35.8	$ 21,988	0.79	83.7%
OXY	Occidental Petroleum	$ 77	4.0%	42.7	2.8	$ 58,564	0.37	2.5%
PAYX	Paychex	$ 68	3.0%	27.7	12.3	$ 24,302	0.99	44.0%
PBCT	People's United	$ 19	3.5%	15.5	1.2	$ 6,745	0.98	6.0%
PCAR	PACCAR	$ 76	1.3%	16.0	3.4	$ 26,863	1.10	19.0%
PCG	PG&E	$ 44	#N/A	11.5	1.2	$ 22,542	-0.17	12.3%
PCLN	Priceline Group	$ 1,919	#N/A	23.0	7.3	$ 93,608	1.55	32.5%
PDCO	Patterson Companies	$ 38	2.8%	17.7	2.6	$ 3,557	0.89	11.3%
PEG	Public Service Enterprise	$ 50	3.4%	16.8	1.9	$ 25,353	0.22	4.0%
PEP	PepsiCo	$ 117	2.7%	20.7	12.6	$	0.63	57.2%

					166,931		
PFE	Pfizer	$ 37	3.7%	13.3	3.6	$ 217,804	1.08 16.3%
PFG	Principal Financial Group	$ 74	2.6%	12.6	1.8	$ 21,428	1.56 16.3%
PG	Procter & Gamble	$ 90	3.1%	21.4	4.2	$ 227,337	0.46 28.6%
PGR	Progressive	$ 56	1.2%	16.6	3.5	$ 32,537	0.87 16.3%
PH	Parker Hannifin	$ 210	1.3%	21.7	5.1	$ 27,983	1.26 21.4%
PHM	PulteGroup	$ 34	1.0%	11.5	2.3	$ 10,136	0.95 14.1%
PKG	Packaging Corp of America	$ 128	2.0%	18.9	6.1	$ 12,107	2.12 27.7%
PKI	PerkinElmer	$ 79	0.4%	22.9	3.4	$ 8,696	1.03 17.4%
PLD	Prologis	$ 62	2.9%	43.8	2.1	$ 32,909	0.93 12.0%
PM	Philip Morris Intl	$ 105	4.1%	19.6	#N/A	$ 162,310	0.76 -58.1%
PNC	PNC Financial Services Gr	$ 152	2.0%	15.1	1.6	$ 72,246	1.02 9.3%
PNR	Pentair	$ 74	1.9%	18.8	2.7	$ 13,395	1.44 13.3%
PNW	Pinnacle West Capital	$ 79	3.5%	18.0	1.7	$ 8,851	0.04 10.6%
PPG	PPG Industries	$ 118	1.5%	17.8	5.1	$ 30,071	1.64 33.6%
PPL	PPL	$ 31	5.1%	13.3	2.0	$	0.34 14.8%

						21,397		
PRGO	Perrigo Co	$ 92	0.7%	17.1	2.1	$ 12,929	0.78	-20.0%
PRU	Prudential Financial	$ 124	2.4%	10.3	1.0	$ 52,627	1.68	8.8%
PSA	Public Storage	$ 194	4.1%	25.5	6.9	$ 33,686	0.37	29.4%
PSX	Phillips 66	$ 105	2.7%	15.5	2.4	$ 53,193	0.96	9.2%
PVH	PVH	$ 144	0.1%	18.4	2.1	$ 11,049	0.55	10.7%
PWR	Quanta Services	$ 39	#N/A	16.1	1.6	$ 6,102	0.74	8.4%
PX	Praxair	$ 164	1.9%	25.7	7.5	$ 46,997	1.18	29.1%
PXD	Pioneer Natural Resources	$ 186	0.0%	48.8	3.0	$ 31,676	1.12	1.2%
PYPL	PayPal Holdings	$ 81	#N/A	35.6	6.3	$ 96,802	#N/A	10.6%
QCOM	Qualcomm	$ 65	3.5%	18.3	3.1	$ 96,381	1.75	7.9%
QRVO	Qorvo	$ 71	#N/A	13.1	1.8	$ 9,033	#N/A	-0.4%
RCL	Royal Caribbean Cruises	$ 128	1.9%	14.8	2.6	$ 27,303	1.18	16.9%
RE	Everest Re Group	$ 224	2.3%	11.0	1.2	$ 9,208	0.42	3.3%
REG	Regency Centers	$ 64	3.3%	44.9	1.7	$ 10,977	0.41	3.1%
REGN	Regeneron Pharmaceuticals	$ 367	#N/A	21.4	6.5	$ 39,426	1.48	25.2%

RF	Regions Financial	$ 18	2.0%	14.6	1.3	$ 21,204	1.61	7.6%
RHI	Robert Half International	$ 56	1.7%	17.7	6.2	$ 7,065	1.39	29.2%
RHT	Red Hat	$ 126	#N/A	43.8	15.6	$ 22,294	1.51	25.3%
RJF	Raymond James Financial	$ 97	1.0%	14.7	2.5	$ 13,977	1.90	12.2%
RL	Ralph Lauren	$ 107	1.9%	18.9	2.5	$ 8,679	0.10	2.3%
RMD	ResMed	$ 88	1.6%	28.8	6.1	$ 12,456	0.82	18.8%
ROK	Rockwell Automation	$ 208	1.6%	27.8	10.0	$ 26,718	1.10	37.3%
ROP	Roper Technologies	$ 275	0.6%	27.2	4.4	$ 28,178	1.36	11.8%
ROST	Ross Stores	$ 84	0.8%	25.3	11.2	$ 31,940	0.97	43.7%
RRC	Range Resources	$ 18	0.5%	21.8	0.8	$ 4,362	0.75	-0.9%
RSG	Republic Services	$ 68	2.0%	25.7	3.0	$ 22,854	0.54	10.5%
RTN	Raytheon	$ 197	1.6%	23.6	5.3	$ 57,083	0.76	20.5%
SBAC	SBA Communications	$ 156	#N/A	97.3	#N/A	$ 18,330	0.99	-5.2%
SBUX	Starbucks	$ 60	2.0%	26.0	15.8	$ 85,937	0.59	50.5%
SCG	SCANA	$ 44	5.6%	15.2	1.1	$ 6,284	-0.16	7.8%
SCHW	Charles Schwab	$ 55	0.6%	23.1	4.9	$ 74,255	2.08	16.0%

SEE	Sealed Air	$ 49	1.3%	19.9	11.6	$ 8,814	0.98	175.5%
SHW	Sherwin-Williams	$ 433	0.8%	23.4	14.8	$ 40,477	1.48	50.5%
SIG	Signet Jewelers	$ 57	2.2%	8.9	1.6	$ 3,446	0.17	21.2%
SJM	JM Smucker	$ 123	2.5%	15.7	2.0	$ 14,021	0.44	8.0%
SLB	Schlumberger	$ 78	2.6%	35.2	2.7	$ 108,009	0.87	1.3%
SLG	SL Green Realty	$ 95	3.4%	50.1	1.4	$ 9,381	1.34	1.7%
SNA	Snap-on	$ 184	1.8%	16.4	3.6	$ 10,466	1.06	20.8%
SNI	Scripps Networks	$ 88	1.4%	16.0	4.3	$ 11,416	1.52	27.1%
SNPS	Synopsys	$ 90	#N/A	25.7	4.1	$ 13,439	1.12	4.1%
SO	Southern	$ 45	5.2%	14.9	1.9	$ 45,003	-0.04	2.4%
SPG	Simon Property Group	$ 166	4.5%	24.4	14.1	$ 51,451	0.60	43.8%
SPGI	S&P Global	$ 178	0.9%	24.6	54.0	$ 45,298	1.45	235.6%
SRCL	Stericycle	$ 72	#N/A	15.9	2.2	$ 6,113	-0.07	-1.0%
SRE	Sempra Energy	$ 107	3.1%	19.3	2.0	$ 26,868	0.52	8.7%
STI	SunTrust Banks	$ 69	2.3%	14.4	1.5	$ 32,794	1.51	8.9%
STT	State Street Corporation	$ 107	1.6%	14.5	2.1	$ 39,769	1.40	12.9%
STX	Seagate	$ 51	4.9%	11.9	11.9	$	1.72	54.1%

	Technology					14,830		
STZ	Constellation Brands	$ 218	1.0%	25.5	5.3	$ 42,354	-0.04	24.8%
SWK	Stanley Black & Decker	$ 173	1.5%	20.7	3.7	$ 26,594	1.27	17.9%
SWKS	Skyworks Solutions	$ 101	1.3%	14.0	4.6	$ 18,541	0.63	26.6%
SYF	Synchrony Financial	$ 39	1.5%	11.3	2.1	$ 30,811	0.91	14.9%
SYK	Stryker	$ 158	1.2%	22.2	5.7	$ 59,216	0.49	18.1%
SYMC	Symantec	$ 29	1.0%	17.2	5.1	$ 17,868	0.98	-6.6%
SYY	Sysco	$ 61	2.4%	21.9	14.3	$ 31,982	0.39	47.7%
T	AT&T	$ 37	5.4%	12.2	1.8	$ 226,529	0.49	10.4%
TAP	Molson Coors Brewing	$ 85	1.9%	16.9	1.5	$ 18,283	0.36	19.5%
TDG	TransDigm Group	$ 293	#N/A	21.7	#N/A	$ 15,198	0.55	-31.7%
TEL	TE Connectivity	$ 100	1.6%	19.0	3.6	$ 35,223	1.10	18.7%
TGT	Target	$ 77	3.2%	16.2	3.7	$ 41,746	0.33	24.0%
TIF	Tiffany	$ 108	1.8%	27.0	4.3	$ 13,479	1.79	15.2%
TJX	TJX Companies	$ 78	1.6%	19.9	10.7	$ 49,497	0.44	53.3%

TMK	Torchmark	$ 92	0.7%	15.7	2.1	$ 10,650	0.97	11.4%
TMO	Thermo Fisher Scientific	$ 210	0.3%	19.8	3.4	$ 84,277	1.00	10.4%
TPR	Tapestry	$ 46	3.0%	19.2	4.4	$ 13,019	0.54	15.9%
TRIP	TripAdvisor	$ 37	#N/A	34.6	3.6	$ 5,075	1.88	4.6%
TROW	T. Rowe Price Group	$ 115	2.0%	16.0	5.1	$ 27,950	1.24	30.0%
TRV	Travelers Companies	$ 135	2.1%	13.2	1.6	$ 36,875	1.19	10.3%
TSCO	Tractor Supply	$ 80	1.4%	20.9	7.3	$ 9,996	1.08	30.9%
TSN	Tyson Foods	$ 80	1.5%	13.6	2.8	$ 29,381	0.35	17.9%
TSS	Total System Services	$ 82	0.6%	21.9	6.4	$ 15,075	1.25	19.1%
TWX	Time Warner	$ 92	1.8%	14.1	2.6	$ 71,669	0.92	16.3%
TXN	Texas Instruments	$ 113	2.2%	24.2	10.1	$ 111,092	1.24	41.3%
TXT	Textron	$ 60	0.1%	20.2	2.7	$ 15,845	1.46	11.1%
UA	Under Armour	$ 14	#N/A	#N/A	3.0	$ 6,246	#N/A	7.1%
UAA	Under Armour	$ 15	#N/A	66.3	3.2	$ 6,678	-0.07	7.1%
UAL	United Continental Holdings	$ 78	#N/A	11.3	2.6	$ 23,226	1.08	22.5%
UDR	UDR	$ 36	3.5%	102.3	3.4	$ 9,559	0.29	10.0%

UHS	Universal Health Services	$ 117	0.3%	14.6	2.3	$ 11,071	0.82	15.1%
ULTA	Ulta Beauty	$ 237	#N/A	28.4	9.0	$ 14,475	0.78	30.9%
UNH	UnitedHealth Group	$ 229	1.3%	20.4	4.9	$ 221,568	0.53	20.9%
UNM	Unum	$ 59	1.6%	11.4	1.4	$ 13,147	1.67	10.6%
UNP	Union Pacific	$ 141	1.9%	19.6	5.8	$ 111,125	1.04	23.2%
UPS	United Parcel Service	$ 134	2.5%	19.0	76.6	$ 115,550	0.82	277.1%
URI	United Rentals	$ 181	#N/A	14.4	6.9	$ 15,299	3.06	33.1%
USB	US Bancorp	$ 57	2.1%	14.2	2.2	$ 94,558	0.96	14.1%
UTX	United Technologies	$ 137	2.1%	19.7	3.7	$ 109,069	1.00	18.1%
V	Visa	$ 120	0.7%	29.1	10.3	$ 280,313	1.06	25.4%
VAR	Varian Medical Systems	$ 108	#N/A	25.6	6.6	$ 9,940	0.76	16.3%
VFC	VF	$ 78	2.4%	22.3	7.8	$ 30,743	0.71	22.3%
VIAB	Viacom	$ 34	2.4%	9.1	2.3	$ 13,580	1.82	37.6%
VLO	Valero Energy	$ 97	2.9%	14.1	2.1	$ 42,336	1.01	10.3%
VMC	Vulcan Materials	$ 134	0.8%	32.3	3.8	$ 17,722	0.91	8.4%

VNO	Vornado Realty Trust	$ 72	3.3%	#N/A	3.9	$ 13,656	1.20 16.1%
VRSK	Verisk Analytics	$ 98	#N/A	27.4	9.6	$ 16,057	0.76 31.4%
VRSN	VeriSign	$ 114	#N/A	26.4	#N/A	$ 11,199	1.14 -38.4%
VRTX	Vertex Pharmaceuticals	$ 158	#N/A	53.1	22.3	$ 39,941	2.08 13.7%
VTR	Ventas	$ 55	5.8%	30.1	1.8	$ 19,528	0.12 11.2%
VZ	Verizon Communications	$ 52	4.6%	13.1	7.9	$ 211,560	0.72 67.2%
WAT	Waters	$ 210	#N/A	26.1	6.3	$ 16,682	1.15 22.6%
WBA	Walgreens Boots Alliance	$ 76	2.1%	13.3	2.9	$ 75,360	0.90 13.4%
WDC	Western Digital	$ 83	2.4%	6.2	2.0	$ 24,586	1.08 12.9%
WEC	WEC Energy Group	$ 64	3.5%	19.4	2.2	$ 20,080	-0.18 10.7%
WFC	Wells Fargo	$ 63	2.5%	13.0	1.7	$ 308,013	1.05 11.9%
WHR	Whirlpool	$ 173	2.6%	11.1	2.6	$ 12,414	1.62 16.6%
WLTW	Willis Towers Watson	$ 155	1.4%	15.9	2.1	$ 20,527	1.02 4.5%
WM	Waste Management	$ 88	1.9%	24.8	7.3	$ 38,328	0.71 25.6%
WMB	Williams Companies	$ 33	3.6%	33.7	3.4	$ 27,456	1.68 6.9%

WMT	Wal-Mart Stores	$ 101	2.0%	22.7	3.9	$ 298,815	0.10	15.0%
WRK	WestRock	$ 69	2.5%	18.2	1.7	$ 17,629	#N/A	7.2%
WU	The Western Union	$ 21	3.3%	11.5	13.7	$ 9,700	0.92	23.7%
WY	Weyerhaeuser	$ 35	3.6%	25.9	2.9	$ 26,615	1.49	9.4%
WYN	Wyndham Worldwide	$ 118	2.0%	16.6	19.1	$ 11,914	1.44	86.7%
WYNN	Wynn Resorts	$ 166	1.2%	24.5	51.7	$ 17,015	2.25	218.2%
XEC	Cimarex Energy	$ 127	0.3%	19.8	5.0	$ 12,111	1.04	16.3%
XEL	Xcel Energy	$ 45	3.2%	18.5	2.0	$ 22,925	-0.04	10.7%
XL	XL Group	$ 35	2.5%	9.6	0.9	$ 9,086	0.76	-2.6%
XLNX	Xilinx	$ 75	1.9%	29.0	7.5	$ 18,736	0.89	24.9%
XOM	Exxon Mobil	$ 88	3.5%	20.5	2.0	$ 370,832	0.69	7.4%
XRAY	Dentsply Sirona	$ 66	0.5%	22.8	2.0	$ 15,111	1.42	-10.1%
XRX	Xerox	$ 33	3.1%	9.3	1.6	$ 8,343	1.06	-8.4%
XYL	Xylem	$ 70	1.0%	25.0	5.1	$ 12,655	0.98	13.5%
YUM	Yum Brands	$ 84	1.4%	26.0	#N/A	$ 28,179	0.65	-23.1%
ZBH	Zimmer Biomet Holdings	$ 122	0.8%	14.9	2.4	$ 24,722	1.13	6.5%

ZION	Zions Bancorp	$ 53	1.2%	15.0	1.5	$ 10,642	1.78	8.6%
ZTS	Zoetis	$ 75	0.7%	26.7	18.5	$ 36,737	1.21	55.9%

The full list of 53 S&P Dividend Aristocrat Companies as of January 25, 2018

1. 3M Company (MMM)

2. AFLAC Inc. (AFL)

3. AbbVie Inc. (ABBV)

4. Abbott Laboratories (ABT)

5. Air Products & Chemicals Inc (APD)

6. A.O. Smith (AOS)

7. Archer-Daniels-Midland Co (ADM)

8. AT&T (T)

9. Automatic Data Processing (ADP)

10. Becton Dickinson (BDX)

11. Brown-Forman (Class B shares BF/B)

12. Cardinal Health Inc. (CAH)

13. Chevron Corp. (CVX)

14. Cincinnati Financial Corp (CINF)

15. Cintas Corp (CTAS)

16. The Clorox Company (CLX)

17. Coca-Cola Co (KO)

18. Colgate-Palmolive (CL)

19. Consolidated Edison Inc (ED)

20. Dover Corp (DOV)

21. Ecolab Inc (ECL)

22. Emerson Electric (EMR)

23. Exxon Mobil Corp (XOM)

24. Federal Realty Investment Trust (FRT)

25. Franklin Resources (BEN)

26. General Dynamics (GD)
27. Genuine Parts Company (GPC)
28. W. W. Grainger (GWW)
29. Hormel Foods Corp (HRL)
30. Illinois Tool Works (ITW)
31. Johnson & Johnson (JNJ)
32. Kimberly-Clark (KMB)
33. Leggett & Platt (LEG)
34. Lowe's Companies, Inc. (LOW)
35. McCormick & Company (MKC)
36. McDonald's (MCD)
37. Medtronic (MDT)
38. Nucor (NUE)
39. PPG Industries (PPG)
40. PepsiCo (PEP)
41. Pentair (PNR)
42. Praxair (PX)
43. Procter & Gamble (PG)
44. Roper Technologies (ROP)
45. S&P Global (formerly McGraw Hill Financial, Inc. SPGI)
46. Sherwin-Williams (SHW)
47. Stanley Black & Decker Inc. (SWK)
48. Sysco (SYY)
49. T. Rowe Price (TROW)
50. Target Corporation (TGT)
51. VF Corporation (VFC)
52. Walmart (WMT)
53. Walgreen Boots Alliance (WBA)

Conclusion

Dividend stock investing is a very reliable passive income and it can help you avoid worrying about after retirement financial stability. Creating and maintaining real wealth through dividend investment requires a long-term investment strategy. This book shows you why you don't have to try to beat the market and how you can use dividends to capture the income and growth you seek.

Autor Bio

A ndrus Istomin is a programmer, book reader and a writer. He is self-employed and works at "Armcon Business Park "IT farm that he established in 2008. Graduated from "London School of Economics and Political Science (LSE)" University; he is passionate about digital currencies and new ways of transaction methods. He understands that electronic currencies are the future, so he is eager to learn about it and want to share his experience with his readers. Andrus interest in literature does not end here. He is a keen observer of the investment market and his new book is on Dividend Investment. Dividend Investment is a reliable passive income opportunity for working people who want a financially secure retirement. In the upcoming months, he plans to publish more books that will bring true value to his readers' lives.

Other books by Andrus Istomin

Bitcoin

Everything You Need to Know about Bitcoin, how to Mine Bitcoin, how to Buy BTC and how to Make Money with Bitcoin.

AN ALIAS SATOSHI NAKAMOTO created Bitcoin, world's first cryptocurrency in 2008. The starting price of Bitcoin was around 2 cents per Bitcoin. In recent years, its growing popularity has caused its value to skyrocket. As of December 2017, the price of each Bitcoin is worth over $15000 and still rising. Over the last five years, Bitcoin investment outperformed popular investment sectors like real estate, gold, and stock. Experts are now saying that the price of 1 single Bitcoin could reach 20k within the next year. Currently, the Bitcoin is functioning as a people's currency, and there is a lot of hype surrounding Bitcoin.

BITCOIN HAS BECOME a buzzword and has a far-reaching global impact. People who invested early on Bitcoin made a fortune, but it doesn't mean latecomers like you can't make a profit. If you are looking for a guide to know what Bitcoin is and how to invest and make a profit, then this Ultimate Bitcoin Guide is for you. This easy-to-read, easy-to-understand guide explains everything the reader needs to know about Bitcoin. This Bitcoin guidebook is for

anyone who doesn't want to be left behind in the next technological revolution.

This book will explain everything that you need to know to get started with Bitcoin. In this book, you will find basic, accurate, detailed information that will help you understand what Bitcoin is. How you can use it to achieve your own needs, wants and goals. Apart from discussing the uses of Bitcoin in everyday life and business, the final chapter discusses a variety of ways you can make a profit with Bitcoin. This book is the asset that will change your views on the financial system, currency and investment. The clock is ticking, so don't take too long. Grab your copy today! Start to read the book and secure your financial fortune.

In this book you will learn:

- Introduction
- Chapter 1 Bitcoin! What is it?
- Chapter 2 Bitcoin and Blockchain
- Chapter 3 Bitcoin Address
- Chapter 4 Buying Your First Bitcoin
- Chapter 5 Using Bitcoin
- Chapter 6 Investing In Bitcoin
- Chapter 7 Doing Business with Bitcoin
- Chapter 8 Bitcoin Mining
- Chapter 9 Security Factor
- Chapter 10 Things You Should Know
- Chapter 11 Make Money with Bitcoin
- Conclusion

Your Free Gift

The free bonus will be waiting for you at this link

H ttps://mavro111.wixsite.com/istomin[1]

[2]

Ethereum For Dummies
Everything You Need to Know About Ethereum, How to Mine Ethereum, How to Exchange Ethereum and How to Buy ETH
Andrus Istomin

Was this book helpful?

"Please leave a review if you enjoyed the book"

Don't miss out!

Visit the website below and you can sign up to receive emails whenever Andru Istomin publishes a new book. There's no charge and no obligation.

https://books2read.com/r/B-A-ZNTE-SSCT

BOOKS 2 READ

Connecting independent readers to independent writers.

Did you love *Automatic Passive Income - How the Best Dividend Stocks Can Generate Passive Income for Wealth Building.*? Then you should read *Blockchain What is Blockchain Technology, Cryptocurrency Bitcoin, Ethereum, and Smart Contracts? Blockchain for dummies.* by Robert Spinelli!

*Are you new to **blockchain technology**? While you might be familiar with Bitcoin and Cryptocurrency, the words - Blockchain and blockchain programming can be intimidating for some. Inside this comprehensive Blockchain for dummies guide, you will acquire all the necessary information that you need. These days, there is a lot of hype surrounding the concept of the blockchain revolution. The industry experts see the technology as one of the greatest innovations since the invention of the internet. Numerous companies, banks, and several governments are rushing to implement blockchain technology in various areas that could*

impact every person on the planet within the next few years. At present Blockchain is the biggest revolution in the financial sector.

Cryptocurrencies might be interesting, but go pale when compared with blockchain technology. Experts predict that the blockchain technology will change the way information is shared across the world, and it will become a central part of our lives over the next ten to fifteen years. What is Blockchain? The blockchain is simple, inexpensive, and effective revolutionary protocol that allows transactions to be secure and anonymous by keeping a hack-proof public ledger of value. The blockchain is a decentralized public ledger, which keeps records of all the transactions on a blockchain network comprising consumers, services, and suppliers of products. Instead of relying on a centralized authority, blockchain technology established a peer-to-peer network through a distributed consensus mechanism.

At its core, a blockchain builds trust into the network, eliminates intermediaries and secure data transaction. Blockchains are new technology layers that revamp the internet. After setup, blockchains never go offline and offer an incredible amount of resiliency. This book will delve into the world of blockchain and give a layman's overview of what it is, how it works and what the future might hold. This guide includes all of the basic information that you need to know about blockchain; what it is; how it was introduced; why it is so important today; and how it can be used in every sector of the contemporary world. Whether you are a private citizen, an inventor or an entrepreneur, blockchain technology is going to mean a lot to you in the future. Over the coming years, you will come to see blockchain technology play an ever greater role in your daily life. Don't get left behind, start to read the book, enlighten yourself and prepare for the future.

Are you new to blockchain technology? While you might be familiar with Bitcoin and Cryptocurrency, the words - Blockchain and blockchain programming can be intimidating for some. Inside this comprehensive Blockchain for dummies guide, you will acquire all the necessary information that you need. These days, there is a lot of hype surrounding the concept of the blockchain revolution. The industry experts see the technology as one of the greatest innovations since the invention of the internet. Numerous companies, banks, and several governments are rushing to implement blockchain technology in various areas that could impact every person on the planet within the next few years. At present Blockchain is the biggest revolution in the financial sector.

Read more...

Also by Andru Istomin

Ethereum For Dummies
Cryptocurrency Mining How To Earn To The Beginner
Cryptocurrency Bitcoin Ethereum Litecoin Dogecoin
Bitcoin: Everything You Need to Know about Bitcoin, how to Mine
Bitcoin, how to Exchange Bitcoin and how to Buy BTC.
What is Cryptocurrency? Everything You Need to Know about
Cryptocurrency; Bitcoin, Ethereum, Litecoin, and Dogecoin
Bitcoin Everything You Need to Know about Bitcoin, how to Mine
Bitcoin, how to Buy BTC and how to Make Money with Bitcoin.
Automatic Passive Income - How the Best Dividend Stocks Can
Generate Passive Income for Wealth Building.

www.ingramcontent.com/pod-product-compliance
Lightning Source LLC
Chambersburg PA
CBHW021846170526
45157CB00007B/2969